NEW
STEPS

PAUL GROVES · **JOHN GRIFFIN**

NATIONAL CURRICULUM · KEY STAGE 3

BOOK 3

Watch your language!

New Steps Book 3 follows the requirements of the National Curriculum up to the end of Key Stage 3, which most of you will achieve at age 14. The book will involve you in many different activities: writing a soap opera, filling in an insurance claim, making a ghost story, being a theatre critic; you will be shown how to use your library more profitably, act in a play, make a *Which?* report on spelling rules, judge a poetry competition. The emphasis is on variety, using many writing and speaking styles on different subjects for different audiences.

But one thing links them all – **language**. This book, and the National Curriculum, is about words, how they fit together to make meanings. Words are tricky things. You think you have them pinned down and they slip away to join others and make new meanings. What, for instance, does the title of this piece mean? It appears to mean 'Look at your words', but people use the phrase most often to mean 'Don't swear!' But 'watch' can also mean 'Take care of', 'Be careful about'. Which meaning is meant here? How do you know?

You know, of course, because of the context, the words in the sentences that follow the title. Words take much of their meaning from other words around them.

You need to interpret words, even the simplest of them have hidden meanings. Here's an example of their subtlety.

What are you doing? Now what are you doing! What do you think you're doing! What are you supposed to be doing? John, what are you doing? What are you doing, John? What are you up to? What do you think you are playing at!

These all appear to mean the same thing. But you are already experienced enough language users to know that some of these mean 'Stop it!' Others you can't be sure about – it depends on the context. And it would help, if you could hear them spoken. How?

In written language we use signs as a guide to the tone of voice. Which ones are used here? Words like 'now', 'think', 'supposed' don't necessarily mean what they appear to mean. How are they used here? And then there's the order of the words to think about. What difference is made by putting 'John' at the beginning of the sentence?

Wouldn't it be much easier if there were fewer words and everybody knew exactly what they meant? Read this passage about a man making a new dictionary.

'How is the dictionary getting on?' said Winston, raising his voice to overcome the noise.

'Slowly,' said Syme. 'I'm on the adjectives. It's fascinating.' Syme had cheered up at the mention of the dictionary. He pushed his bowl of pinkish stew aside, took up a hunk of bread in one hand and a sweaty lump of cheese in the other and leaned across the table so he could speak without shouting.

'This edition is the eleventh and, I think, the last. We're getting the language into its final shape – the shape it's going to have when nobody speaks anything else. When we've finished, people like you will have to learn the language all over again. I daresay you think our main job is inventing new words. But not a bit of it. We're destroying words – scores of them, hundreds of them, every day. We're cutting the language down to the bone. It's a beautiful thing, the destruction of words. Of course, it's easiest to get rid of verbs and adjectives, but there are hundreds of nouns that can be got rid of as well. The synonyms are easy, of course. Do you know that there are over twenty words to express the idea of walking, and at least as many for speaking? Obviously we've cut all those out. But the antonyms are just as unnecessary. After all, why do you need a word that is the opposite of another word? Take 'good', for instance. If you have a word like good, what need is there for a word like 'bad'? 'Ungood' will do just as well – better, really, because it's the exact opposite, which the other is not. Or, if you want a stronger version of 'good', what sense is there in having a whole string of useless words like 'excellent' and 'splendid' and all the rest of them? 'Plusgood' covers the meaning or 'doubleplusgood' if you want something stronger still. When we've finished, the whole idea of 'good' and 'bad' will be covered by one word. Don't you see the beauty of that, Winston?'

'Oh, yes,' said Winston, twitching out a smile, but in truth upset not only by the idea of word-destruction, but by having soon, if Syme was right, only 'doubleplusungood' to show, or even think, his opposition.

Syme noticed Winston's lack of enthusiasm. 'Don't you see,' he said, 'that our aim is to narrow the range of thought? In the end criminal thoughts will be impossible because there will be no words to express them. For instance, we're cutting out unnecessary words such as 'freedom', the idea of being free to choose – when the word has gone, so has the idea. The process will continue long after you and I are dead. Every year fewer and fewer words, so every year the range of thought smaller and smaller. It's a wonderful idea. Of course, it was Big Brother's idea in the first place.'

'Of course,' said Winston.

Adapted from *Nineteen Eighty-Four* by George Orwell

How would you like to live in the world of Syme, Winston, and Big Brother? Perhaps you've heard of Big Brother and the novel *Nineteen Eighty-Four* by George Orwell. It's a nightmare idea of the future, where you're watched by telescreens and listened to by hidden microphones wherever you go. The slightest sign of rebellion against Big Brother will take you to the Ministry of Love, where you're tortured or shot! You're not allowed even to think disobedience. How can they stop you? Well, Syme is working on one of the ways; the compilers of the new dictionary are taking away words that Big Brother doesn't approve of. If you only know his words, you can only think his way. Think for yourself about this. Can you think without language? And, if you can't think your own thoughts, are you a person at all?

George Orwell thought language sufficiently important to make getting rid of words part of his nightmare world, a world where meanings are as clear as mathematical symbols, an awful world.

Watch your language!

Contents

LANGUAGE
ROOTS

1

The main aim of the National Curriculum is to make you think about language, to treasure the language you have inherited and to use it correctly.

In this Step we look at a story that makes you think about the very roots of language. We also ask you to invent words and to appreciate the sound of words.

Thinking about language

The first thing you need to know about the National Curriculum is that there are ten subjects for you to study. Here they are:

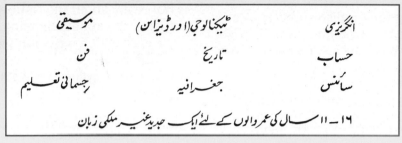

Do you take all these at the moment? You don't know what they are? If you haven't an Urdu speaker in your class, you won't. Try it in Chinese:

```
英文  科技（及設計）  音樂
數學  歷史          藝術
科學  地理          體育
爲十一至十六歲學童而設的一種現代外語。
```

Still no good? Well surely you can manage Turkish:

İngilizce	Teknoloji (ve dizayn)	Müzik
Matematik	Tarih	Sanat
Bilim	Coğrafya	Beden Eğitimi
11—16 yaş arasındakiler için bir Modern Yabancı dil.		

The code is still well out of your grasp. But it doesn't look quite so incomprehensible. Why not? Try this code of written language:

English	Technology (and design)	Music
Mathematics	History	Art
Science	Geography	Physical education
A modern foreign language for 11-16 year olds		

Now there's a code you have cracked. Look again at the Urdu and the Chinese. Unless English is not your first language that is how the first page of your first sight of an English book would look.
What an amazing amount you've learnt already!

⊂⊃ On your own, copy out an Urdu word. Show it to your neighbour. Can he or she even tell which one you've written? That's how it felt when you were copying your name for the first time.

⊂⊃ Now using the English subjects as a guide write the Urdu, Chinese and Turkish words for 'Mathematics'. Are you sure you have the right ones?

One of the first things you learnt about your own language code was to read it from left to right. Why not right to left, or even bottom to top?

Of course, you will have got the right Turkish word. What feature do English and Turkish have in common? Perhaps you know the German, French or Spanish for Mathematics. They have the same feature. And some of the names of subjects look the same. Why? The answer lies partly in history and geography. In what ways? Discuss this with your teacher.

How our code has changed

By now you will have guessed that this Step is not really about the National Curriculum subjects. It's about language, the written code with which we communicate with each other. The code you are studying in this book is English. Let's start with a piece of poetry.

Da com of more under misthleopurn Grendel gongan Godes yrre boer.

What do you think of it so far? Rubbish? Perhaps you will understand this version better.

Then from the moor under the misty cliffs Came Grendel, he bore God's anger.

Both pieces are written in English – the first one over a thousand years ago!

Compare it with the modern version and you can see the connections. What are they? How has the code altered over the years? Notice how *misty cliffs* are all one word in the first version. On the other hand *came* is two words – separated in the sentence. Which two? Look at *gongan*. Any Geordies amongst you will know the word. In German 'gegangen' means 'went' – the opposite of 'came'. But Grendel (he's a monster!) 'went' from under the cliffs means the same as 'came'. And isn't our word 'going' connected?

There's only one word in the **Old English** (or Anglo-Saxon) that looks totally foreign – *yrre*. Look up 'ire' in your dictionary. After the definition it will tell you what language it is from.

This gives you some idea of the intermingling and development of language.

Finally, try another poem in English.

A povre wydwe somdeel stape in age ·
Was whilom dwellyng in a narwe cotage
Biside a grove standynge in a dale
This wydwe, of which I telle you my tale
Syn thilke day that she was last a wyf
In pacience ladde a ful symple lyf.

You don't need much help with this – it's only 600 years old – **Middle English**.

▭ See if you can translate it into modern English. Do as much as you can before seeking help from your teacher.

▭ In small groups, discuss the following. See how much agreement you can come to about these questions.

1 What is language?
2 How did language begin?
3 What would be lost without language?
4 How does language spread and change?
5 What 'different' kinds of English are there?

Now come together as a class and pool your ideas.

FOOTNOTE

However a written language works, it will always be based on naming words (*nouns*). Part of the English code is to indicate certain nouns by the use of *capital letters – proper nouns*. (We also use capital letters for any word beginning a sentence.) Use this Step to revise proper nouns. Make a list of twenty, saying what category they come under, e.g. names of people, towns, etc.

A piece of research about language

▭ Break up into small groups and read the sad little tale on page 12. Do the same rules about capital letters seem to have applied when this was written? Can you find any consistent use of capitals here? In what striking way does this passage differ from a modern English version?

A

SHORT, but concise account of ELISABETH and MARY CHULKHURST, who were born joined together by the Hips and Shoulders, in the Year of our Lord 1100, at BIDDENDEN, in the COUNTY of KENT;

COMMONLY CALLED THE

Biddenden Maids.

THE Reader will obferve by the above Plate of them, that they lived together in the above ftate, Thirty-four Years; at the expiration of which Time, one of them was taken Ill, and in a fhort time died; the furviving one was advifed to be feparated from the body of her deceafed Sifter, by diffection, but fhe abfolutely refufed the feparation, by faying thefe words, as we came together, we will alfo go together, and in the fpace of about fix hours after her Sifter's deceafe, She was taken Ill, and died alfo.

BY their WILL, they bequeathed to the *Churchwardens* of the Parifh of BIDDENDEN, and their fucceffors *Churchwardens* for ever, certain pieces or parcels of Land in the Parifh of *Biddenden* containing twenty Acres, more or lefs, which now lets at £.31 10s. *per Annum.* There are ufually made in commemoration of thefe wonderful phænomena's of nature, about 1000 Rolls with their impreffion printed on them, and given away to all Strangers, on *Eafter Sunday*, after Divine Service in the Afternoon; alfo about 300 Quartern Loaves, and Cheefe in proportion, to all the poor Inhabitants of the faid Parifh.

Cracking the code

Now read this story, which should get you thinking about language.

Homework

The following story is for dictionary practice.

With these worksheets take a dictionary home from your form cupboard.

The most difficult words in the story are underlined. For each of these words find the correct dictionary meaning and write it in pencil above the word. Then try and read the sentence in which the words occur and try and understand the whole sentence.

Tomorrow in class there will be a spelling test on some of these hard words.

Many civilisations known to man have perished. Under the city of Jerusalem, for instance, there are buried nine cities. Each of these nine cities belong to an age of the human habitation that flourished at one time on that spot. We can learn about the way the people behind these civilisations lived by examining the things they left behind. At different times in human history, people spoke and wrote different languages. Archaeologists have set themselves the task of deciphering these languages, many of which are related to the languages we speak and write today. Some of them are dead languages: which means that no living person knows them. Yet we have some knowledge of how those people lived by codifying their scripts.

Some civilisations, however, have left no trace except that of legend. The ancient Greeks believed, for instance, that there was a civilisation that had been swept under the sea by natural factors and had continued under water. They called this civilisation Atlantis. Modern scientists have tried to find out when and where Atlantis existed, but without much convincing success.

It is easy, however, to imagine a civilisation of the past which had no written script. The people may and will have talked to each other but will have left no record of their language in written form. Today we feel that the absence of a written script would be a tragedy. We would not, without writing, be able to transmit everything we know to people who come after us. Our sciences would then become extinct.

Imagine, for instance, that twenty five years from the day you read this story, the world is destroyed. It may be destroyed by human agency, such as nuclear warfare, or it may be destroyed, as perhaps was Atlantis, by natural disaster, or in fact by a combination of both.

According to one American scientist, that is not such a remote possibility. He says that our factories are putting out smoke in such density that our planet is under sentence of death. His hypothesis is that the hot smoke rises and forms a layer above the earth. This layer destroys another layer of gas that protects the earth from the full heat of the sun's rays. If the full heat of the sun were to play on the snows of the Arctic and the Antarctic, it would melt the snows of those regions. The melted snow would flow into the oceans and the flood that would ensue would make the flood of Noah look like a puddle in summer rain.

After this flood there will be silence. None of the countries and land that we know will survive, except perhaps the highest peaks in the world. Today those high peaks, such as Mount Everest in the Himalayas in India, are cold and snowbound.

If you imagine a world after this terrible flood, the snow on these peaks will melt. The valleys around them will be flooded and will become part of the oceans and only people who make their way up to the high peaks will survive. They will live on a group of rugged islands surrounded by the sea.

Do these people believe in Gods? Of course they don't. They know very little of what we knew, because they could carry very little of the objects of their environment when they escaped the flood. They are people who have foreseen the destruction of our world. Do they want to build the same world, believe in the same things again? Of course they don't. They want to forget about the science and the industry and the factories and the manufacture that have brought about the world's watery end. So with them they take only the essentials that nature will foster. They take seeds and trees and a few animals.

Their civilisation grows. When the trees mature and yield wood, they build boats. They make tools by striking stone against stone. Their children and their children's children believe in the sunrise and the sunset and the heat of the day and the fresh of the night and are never told about the humans that went before them.

They learn instead the arts of the primitive maritime peoples. How to skin a fish and use its bones as hooks, how to tell the regular ebb and flow of the tides. Through generations they are happy and oblivious of the twentieth century and our factories and our wars and our cities and our schools and our jails and our jealousies.

Amongst one generation of these new people of Everest is a boy called Zal. He goes fishing with his father and the other men of the tribe. He knows all about hooks and bait. Several times in his life he has been dragged off one of the little crafts of the islanders to fight with some monster of the deep, stab it and swim to the surface to ask the assistance of his companions in bringing up his kill from the sea. He swims like a creature with webbed feet, one that can hold its breath underwater for several minutes. He has learnt this skill from childhood, because it is necessary to jump overboard and lure the carnivorous fish by using yourself as human bait.

One day the men in the boat throw Zal over the side and wait for him to rise like a bubble in a bottle of pop. He waves to them, several feet away now, and they throw out the line weighted with a stone that sinks faster than the fish he has killed. It is Zal's task to tangle the body of the fish in this line. It is a great big fish, of a kind that Zal has never seen before. A magnificent catch.

They trail the fish and row back to the island once Zal is safely back in the boat. They pull it up on the beach and require six men to drag the hauling line.

It is Zal's fish. He has the first knife cut. He slits the belly of the fish, cuts its fins and breaks its jaw with a stone. He wants to keep its teeth as souvenirs. The people of his village gather round as he explores the anatomy of this unknown variety of sea monster. Its blood is as wine-red and watery as that of any other fish, but in its belly it contains a strange sack. It is black and thick like the skin of an animal. Zal examines this strange stomach, like an inner stomach. Down one side it has little teeth clamped together which shine like the sun on the waters at dawn. Hard teeth they are too.

'This one has two stomachs and teeth inside its belly too,' Zal says.

'Divide the meat,' says one of the elders impatiently. 'You can keep the inner teeth as a souvenir too.'

'I've seen such a monster before,' says another elder. 'My grandfather captured one. He said they live forever unless a hunter catches them. That one had no second stomach like this.'

Zal cuts the rest of the innards of the fish and offers the body to the village. The custom of their village is that they take equal shares of the day's catch.

Then an elder steps forward and says, 'Let me have a look at that inner stomach. The fish may be poisonous.'

Zal hands the rectangular sack over to the elder.

'Never seen anything like it. I would be very careful about eating the flesh of this one. I feel Zal has caught a poisonous monster. Look at this stomach lining, it's rough and black and oily.'

There is a murmur amongst the gathering. A woman speaks out saying that she will not risk taking a piece of Zal's fish home. Others agree.

The gathering moves on to the smaller catches of the day. Zal sits on the ground by his catch. This is unfortunate. It is the biggest fish he has ever caught. Now the people of the village will just leave it there, lying gutted and open like a collapsed tent, its skin resting on the sand, its eye bulgy and misty.

Zal looks down the broken jaw of his prize. The fish has a huge gullet and the inside of its mouth is ribbed like the bottom of a boat, its palate like the white and green and shady red smoothness of some seashells. He gazes long into the fish's mouth. He doesn't notice that one of the elders has come back and is looking over his shoulder. He turns round when he feels a presence.

'The biggest fish you ever caught, isn't it?' the old man says.

'I don't think it's poisonous,' Zal replies.

'Dorjay says it is an inner stomach, but it's some kind of octopus that the fish has swallowed, I think,' the old man says, and he asks Zal to pass him the black sack. The old man examines it for a few seconds and then throws it on the sand next to the guts of the fish.

'I'm sorry for you boy, but you mustn't be disappointed. You have long to

live. There will be other fish and much appreciation.'

'I suppose so,' Zal says.

When the old man has gone, Zal turns to the black sack, the inner stomach, of the creature the fish has swallowed whole. He picks it up and looks at its teeth. It is made of a substance he has never before seen in a sea creature. He thinks he'll pry open the teeth. He wrenches at them and pulls them apart, but they are shut tight. He runs his finger along the ridge of the teeth and then he notices that at the end of the row of teeth is a loose one. He pulls at that and as if by magic it unlocks the row of teeth, two by two, right down the row, and the mouth of the creature lies gaping in front of him. This thing is more fascinating than the fish itself, he thinks.

Then it occurs to him that this isn't another fish creature, it is some sort of trap, some sort of net without holes. He has often wondered whether fish have any intelligence as humans do and whether they build traps for each other. But he has always put the thought aside. The shape and form of this trap seems to confirm it. He looks into the sack. If this is a creature, it has no head, no gullet, no stomach. Inside, Zal can see something. The inner skin of the trap is dry and in the bottom of it there is a creature. An animal the trap has caught, Zal thinks. He turns the trap upside down and with a jerk upsets the strange animal on to the sands.

It falls, as though on its mouth, and its jaw stretches open, biting the sands. Zal keeps his distance, wary lest the animal still be alive. He walks closer to it. It is curious, this process of <u>intussusception</u> by which the black creature has <u>ingested</u> this one and the fish has swallowed the black creature.

The creature on the sand lies still, making no move to crunch the sand or crawl away. It looks dangerous. It has a rectangular body, no fins or feet and it looks to Zal as though it is nothing but an open jaw. Zal bends over and puts his head on the sand and looks at the creature. It seems to him to have no teeth but has a thousand white tongues which stretch from its spine. It is like a flat clam. An enormous one, but dead.

Zal wants to make sure. He takes his knife from his belt and pokes the creature. It doesn't move. Now he feels bold and grasps it by its spine and lifts it up. The shell and the tongues flap shut. As Zal lifts it, six or eight of the tongues fall out and strew themselves on the sand. Zal puts the creature down and examines these. They are funny. They are smooth and white and rectangular and have a million black markings on each, markings in regular rows such as Zal has never seen.

Now he picks up the creature and flips its tongues. He runs his thumb along the edges of the tongues. They are as smooth as any skin and they too have markings on them, row upon row. The rows of black markings remind Zal of the regularity of a wheat field, or the rows of tiny fish they lay out all over the beach to dry in the sun.

It is miraculous. On every tongue there are two columns of little back markings. There is an <u>intrinsic</u> design to this creature like nothing he's ever seen. Zal tries to dig his nails into the creature's shell which he now sees is a very dark blue, nearly black, like the ocean on some dark night.

For a few hours he sits looking at the signs on the tongues of this unknown creature. Then he buries it in the sand further up the beach. He will keep his discovery a secret. But how will he find the place where he's buried it again? An idea strikes Zal. He will mark the spot with little signs. He takes his knife out and makes several signs on the spot in the sand. Then he notices that he hasn't buried the loose tongues with the creature. He picks those up. He can bend them easily. He rolls them up, as leaves of the banana tree are rolled around fish to cook them, and he takes them home.

At home he examines the signs and markings on the loose tongues. They may not be tongues, Zal thinks, they may be smaller creatures of the same sort that the bigger creature with the shell swallowed.

Zal keeps his secret and every day when he is on his own he goes and digs up the creature and gazes at it. Then slowly it comes to him. On the tongues of the creature are signs such as he himself made on the sands. The regularity of the signs amazes him. There are darker ones and lighter ones, and soon Zal discovers that they are repeated every so often in one row. It reminds him of the knots that fishermen make in thousands to constitute a net.

It is when he is sitting on the beach with other boys and girls of his age one day and being instructed by the elders in the songs of their forefathers, that a thought strikes Zal like a thunderclap. The thought goes round and round in his head. The boy sitting next to him nudges him.

'Zal.'

He looks up at the elder.

'I asked you a question, Zal.'

'Yes sir. What was it? I was thinking.'

'Day dreaming, child.'

The other children laugh.

'I asked you to repeat the song you memorised yesterday.'

'Yes sir.'

'Well?'

'I've forgotten, sir.'

'Forgotten? I don't understand, Zal. Do you forget to eat or to take your share from the day's catch?'

'Once I go away, I forget,' Zal says.

'That's no crime. But couldn't you have asked someone else? The words are easy. It's part of your homework.'

'There must be some other way of remembering, sir,' Zal says.

'What other way, child, except constant repetition and passing on what you know so that knowledge may be shared.'

'Well, sir, I was just thinking. If we had a sign for all the words we speak, one different sign for each word, then we could . . .'

'Yes,' says the elder, 'and if we had a name for every fish that lived in the sea we wouldn't have to catch them, we could call them out by shouting their names.'

The rest of the children laugh.

'No fishing trips for you for a week,' the elder says. 'Now listen while I ask someone else to repeat yesterday's song. Your mind is not on your work. Or it's like a net with larger holes than the fish.'

For a week Zal isn't allowed on to the boats. He feels hurt by the punishment. He makes sure he has learnt the song by doing exactly as he had suggested to the elder. While sitting on the sands, he makes little signs for the words of the song and the next day he comes back and finds the signs in the same order.

The more Zal thinks about it, the more he is convinced. Every day he looks at his captive creature of the tongues. If by some chance, he thinks, by some design, the signs on the flat tongues of the creature have been arranged there by some creature like himself capable of making signs in the sand and each of the signs . . . But no, it is too improbable to even contemplate.

Though he puts this thought out of his head, Zal still examines the signs in the creature for their regularity. In a few months' time he finds, by carefully tracing the signs on the sand next to him as he leafs through the tongues, that there are about seventy signs. Thick ones and thin ones, slanting ones and vertical ones. Soon Zal is able to copy on the sands whole rows of the signs. But he can never know what they mean. When he copies the signs in the sand with his knife, or carves them on palm leaves, he notices that he can never get them as straight and neat as the rows of signs on the creature's tongues. No matter how hard he tries, all he can make are squiggly imitations.

That's why they couldn't have been made by creatures like me, Zal thinks. They are too regular. And yet on the loose tongues that he found, eight of them, there are squiggly signs like Zal's. They are inscribed above other signs with dark black lines under them. Slowly Zal learns to imitate all the signs on these loose tongues. They begin like this:

Homework

The following story is for dictionary practice.

With these worksheets take a dictionary home from your form cupboard.

The most difficult words in the story are underlined. For

And then at the end, on the blank part of the tongue, are these squiggly signs, definite indications that someone like Zal could have made them: *Stuff this, this is boring.*

The story takes you into a world without a written language. But before it does so, it explains

1 what a language is,
2 how we can learn about an extinct civilization from a dead language,
3 what disadvantages a civilization without a written language would suffer from,
4 how another civilization without a written language could still happen,
5 why that civilization might reject a written language.

These things are explained to you through the medium of a written language, a particular code called English. Zal is trying to crack the code. Think of the advantages you have over him, that you have learnt already. You know the code is in a book, that it is trying to tell you something. You can interpret most of the marks. Some, possibly the underlined ones, still escape you. Unlike Zal, you have a code-cracker – a dictionary. You're also sitting next to a code-cracker who might know some of the marks you don't – and vice-versa. There's an expert code-cracker in the room with you – she or he is there to help.

▷ Making use of all these tools available to you explain, in the written language you are familiar with (your own words), what you can learn from the story about numbers 1–5 above.

(And don't write: *Stuff this, it's boring!* The story isn't boring, only the use it was being put to.)

Zal's world

Zal needs to know about how to catch fish and prepare them to eat. He learns songs and plays games. It is enough, for his world. Only fish come out of the sea. Therefore, the zipped bag and the book are part of the fish or animal it has swallowed.

▷ Imagine some other object from the modern world in the fish's stomach. How would Zal approach it, describe it, and what would he think it was? Write about it as if you were Zal. See if your neighbour can guess what it is.

▷ The writer suggests Zal was better off without a written language. Why might this be so? Do you agree? Discuss this in class.

Zal's invention

'There must be some other way of
    remembering, sir.'
'If we had a sign for all the words we speak
    . . .'

Zal is laughed at by his teacher. But he is beginning to think of a written language. Then he makes one to remember the song. What would it look like? The first four lines of Zal's song are:

Under the sea lives a monster fish
A fish that is bigger than the biggest man
One day I'll take my boat to sea
And I'll catch the monster fish

▷ On your own, make the code that will help you remember the words. It can include simple drawings but not English words. Compare your signs with your neighbour's.
Now decide which code is better – or make a combination of the two. You will then have a common language, one you could develop for communication.

FOOTNOTE

One feature of the English code is its use of different types of words in sentences. You probably know most of them: *noun, pronoun, adjective, verb, adverb, conjunction, preposition*. These are called *parts of speech* and each has a different job (function) in an English sentence. You don't have to have divisions in a language, though. For instance, adjectives are describing words: *old, fat, thin, fierce, ugly*, and *graceful* are adjectives that could be used to describe a man. If you wanted to invent a language without adjectives you would need more nouns.

▷ Invent six nouns for the six adjectives applying to 'man'. For instance, *buggle* could mean 'ugly man'. *Lapple* might mean 'graceful man'. Find six words where the sound suits the meaning of the adjective. Perhaps you could use a common ending – in the two nouns above the *le* sound would signify 'man' for instance.

▷ Here are six of the underlined words from the story. Make them into three groups of two by looking at their function in the sentence they are in. How can you check in a dictionary that you have chosen correctly?

    habitat
    flourished
    remote
    primitive
    environment
    ingested

You were asked to make the sound of the six nouns you chose for 'man' to suit the sense.

If you manage to do this your words would be partly:
    onomatopoeic (this word is an adjective).
They would be examples of
    onomatopoeia (this word is a noun. It's meaning is a word or a group of words that suggest the sound they represent).

Some of the first words you learned as a child would be onomatopoeic, e.g. *wuff, miaow, moo*.

▷ Add twenty words to this list of onomatopeic words: *thud, clang, cuckoo* . . .

Here's a famous eighteenth century poet, Alexander Pope, telling us how important the sounds of words are.

It's not enough no Harshness gives offence
The Sound must seem the echo of the
    Sense.
Soft is the strain when Zephyr gently blows
And the smooth stream in smoother
    Numbers flows.
When Ajax strives some rock's vast weight
    to throw,
The line, too, labours and the Words move
    slow.
Not so, when swift Camilla scours the Plain
Flies o're the unbending Corn and skims
along the Main.

Zephyr – *slight wind*
Numbers – *rhythm*
Ajax – *a god*
Camilla – *a goddess*

▷ Look at the verse carefully. How is the smoothness of lines 3 and 4 achieved?
How are lines 5 and 6 made to read like a struggle?
How is the speed of lines 7 and 8 achieved?

WRITING A
SOAP OPERA

2

You can hardly pick up a newspaper these days without reading about *soap* – not the washing kind.
Here we ask you to make your own soap. As well as learning more about them you will also learn a great deal about writing plots and creating characters for fiction.

Introducing soap operas

Soaps got their name from American TV when stories about families and their intrigues were sponsored by soap washing powder firms who actively used the programmes to advertise their products. It now means any series on TV which is about families, groups, neighbourhoods and their doings. The most popular in England at the time of writing this book are *Eastenders*, *Neighbours* and *Coronation Street* which is watched by up to 20 million people each week. Children are avid watchers.
In America the TV audience seems to prefer soaps about rich people living lives the ordinary person can only dream about. In Britain we seem to prefer soaps about ordinary people as in *Coronation Street*.
In this Step we want you to think about the problems of making soaps and to write one of your own. After all, they can be about people you know: your family, friends and neighbours. You have to write little plays about their lives, but as you will see there are differences from writing other plays.

▷ List all the soaps that can be seen on TV at the moment. Say briefly where each one is set and the main things that are going on in them at the moment. You may have to swap information or look in a newspaper or magazine to do this.

The following situation is the one you are going to use for your own soap. It is provisionally called 'B+B'.

B and B

Avril Benson has won a large sum of money on the Pools. She and her husband, Tony, have decided to buy a bed and breakfast guest house in the village of Dalethorpe, a seaside village, two miles from Oxington, a seaside town.

Their two children, Bernie, thirteen and Rebecca, fourteen are not keen to leave their friends and the big city they come from. They think Dalethorpe will be very dull.

Avril's parents are coming as well as there is a granny flat attached to the guest house. Her father, Bill Oakley, is not keen on leaving his council house and bowls club, but his wife, Annie, thinks her life will be transformed by meeting lots of new people.

The last owner failed to make a go of the guest house and it is difficult to attract custom in the winter, but Avril thinks she can be successful by specialising in her hobby of fine English cooking.

There is a shop next door run by an Indian family, the Desais. They have two teenage children as well, Aziz and Saila.

The school all the children will attend will be a comprehensive in Oxington.

The plan is to have stories about the two families and their children, but they are to be interwoven with stories about the guests who have bed and breakfast.

▭ When a company launches a new product they often employ an agency to think of possible names for it. A committee from the company then picks one name which they think will give the product the right image.

In small groups, do the following:

GROUP A: thinks of names for the soap. 'B and B' has been suggested but other names could be better.

GROUP B: thinks up names for the characters, if you don't like the ones already picked.

GROUP C: thinks up names for the village, town and the surrounding area. Once again, the names already used are only suggestions.

GROUP D: thinks up names for the guest house and the shop.

GROUP E: thinks up names for the comprehensive school.

An introductory episode

You need to gradually introduce all the characters and set up some story lines. Here is an introductory *episode*:

> Hall of the guest house. Camera pans round to entrance. A car is heard to stop outside. We hear feet, voices and a key in the lock. The door is thrown open.

TONY Shall I carry you over the threshold?

AVRIL Don't be silly.

TONY We may have been silly, buying this place.

AVRIL It was a joint decision.

BERNIE (Entering) It smells.

AVRIL That's only because it has been empty for six months. The surveyor said it was sound.

REBECCA (Entering) It's filthy.

AVRIL Yes, that will be our first task – decorating.

BERNIE Our?

AVRIL I expect you all to lend a hand.

BERNIE The village looks a dump!

TONY I think you'll like Oxington. And we are by the sea.

REBECCA Big deal. Angela and I both cried when I left.

AVRIL She can come down here on a holiday. We've plenty of beds.

REBECCA She was the best friend I ever had.

AVRIL You'll make lots of new friends.

REBECCA I don't want new friends. I want Angela.

TONY Where's Grandad?

AVRIL I thought they were right behind us at that roundabout.

TONY I wonder if he took the wrong turning?

▭ In small groups, complete some of this episode. Have Gran and Grandad got lost? When do they arrive? The family explore the rest of the house. What are the kids' comments? What problems do they find? Do any neighbours call in to welcome them?

▭ In pairs, here are some practice scenes to write. Write about a page.

1 In bed, Avril and Tony discuss the children's lack of enthusiasm for the move. Have they done the right thing?
2 Avril tries to interest Rebecca in planning the decoration of the guest house.
3 Bernie meets Aziz, the boy in the shop next door owned by Mr Desai. Aziz tells him about school.
4 Grandad says he is going back home to his council house and his allotment. Gran calms him down.
5 A woman arrives urgently needing accommodation. Avril explains that they are not open yet. But what can be done to help the woman?

Locations and sets

The producer says you can have two main outdoor locations which will have to be built.
1 The street with the guest house and the shop next door.
2 The school yard.
Occasionally you may film in real outside locations like the garden of the guest house, Oxington beach, etc.

You may have a variety of indoor sets such as the dining room, the children's rooms, the shop, the classroom, a cafe, etc.

Remember it is cheaper to shoot indoors rather than out where the weather can affect shooting schedules.

Plan the sets

⟹ You have been asked to do the following:

1 Describe and draw plans of the street with the guest house and the school yard.
2 Describe and do a ground plan for a) the inside of the shop; b) the dining room; c) the grandparents' flat d) a set you think will be useful, e.g. a classroom.

The character file

A play or a soap works because all the characters are different, just as people are in real life. Because there are many episodes in a soap you have to make sure your characters behave consistently. To help you as a writer in this task you need to keep a file on each character. Here is one for you:

✳✳✳✳✳✳✳✳✳✳✳✳✳✳✳✳✳✳✳✳✳✳✳✳✳✳✳✳

Avril Benson

Age: 39
Birthday: 3rd October
Height: 5′ 4″, slim build
Complexion: Fair skin with blue eyes. Blonde.
Dress: Likes to dress casually in jeans, but has good dress sense.
Temperament: Easy-going but has a fierce temper when roused. Not as strict with the children as Tony. Seems to like Bernie more than Rebecca, which could lead to problems. Tends to be overconfident about the business. Trying to give up smoking. Likes to be popular with the guests.

✳✳✳✳✳✳✳✳✳✳✳✳✳✳✳✳✳✳✳✳✳✳✳✳✳✳✳✳

You will need to leave space in each file as the characters will develop according to what happens to them in each episode. You will also add likes and dislikes, weaknesses, etc.

⟹ Begin character files for: Tony, Rebecca, Bernie, the grandparents, Aziz and Saila.
As you bring in other characters you will need to create a character file for them.

Casting

⇨ You might like to cast actors and actresses you see on TV or film for your soap. If you do not know their real names, use the characters they play. A real casting director would spend months getting the right people. You may like to cast people in your school or neighbourhood for the young people in your soap.

Storylines

On the credits for a soap you will see the names of the people who thought up the storylines. They are normally different from the writers who write the episodes.

⇨ In small groups, think up storylines for 'B and B'. You will need plenty of arguments, scandal and dramatic happenings. If the characters agree all the time or nothing exciting happens you will not get many viewers.
Look at these possibilities:

1 The children. Do they continue to be unhappy? There is more to write about, if they do. Do they make friends with the Desais? What is their first day at school like? Do they clash with teachers?

2 Is the guest house able to open on time ? What problems of decorating, furnishing and plumbing do the Bensons have? Do Avril and Tony fall out over anything?

3 Where have the Bensons come from? Do they have a different dialect from the local people? Are they accepted at first in the village? There could be a nosey neighbour. Do they get their supplies from the Desais?

4 Does Gran interfere in the guest house? She is very keen to play her full part. How does she deal with a grumpy husband? He could go missing.

5 What succession of guests come to stay? Some should be odd or mysterious. They could come from different classes of society . . .

6 What current issues can you put in your soap to make it topical?

In a full half-hour soap the idea is to switch quickly from scene to scene so as to keep the viewers involved. A scene could last only a minute. You may have as many as twenty scenes in an episode with up to four storylines running. Plan, in note form, a complete episode.

Cliff-hangers

You will need to end each episode of the soap on what is known as a *cliff-hanger*. This means a situation which the audience will want to know the outcome of, like a main character crashing into a tree in a car. This ensures the viewers will switch on next time. The main soaps have little cliff-hangers and then every now and again a big one.

Camera shots

The director needs to know the best camera shots and angles to use in any episode. He or she can use these kind of shots:

Close-up: the head and neck
Medium shot: up to about 9 metres, e.g. inside the Desai's shop
Long shot: as far as the camera can see, e.g. the street outside
2 shot: two characters in shot
3 shot: three characters in shot
O-shot: shot over one character's shoulder to another

Other useful terms are:

Pan: camera moves to right or left
Zoom: camera moves in closer
Cut: end scene

▭▷ In small groups, take two scenes you have written and put in the camera shots on the left of your script. You may need to write the scripts out again leaving plenty of space.
Remember, good camera work can make an episode exciting. If you are finding this difficult, look at any soap on TV and think of it as a group of camera shots.

Selling your soap opera

As well as writing a soap, it is also important to think about ways to sell it.

The theme music

▭▷ If there is a musical member of your group you may like to think about making up the theme music. It can have words (lyrics) or not.

Publicity

You will need to publicise your soap to ensure an initial big audience. This can be done on TV and in the Press.

▭▷ Decide how you are going to publicise your soap. What bits of scenes that you have written would you show to whet the appetite of the public? On TV you would need to put several bits together with a voice-over to link them:

voice-over: 'Coming next week on Tuesday and Thursday. 'B and B', a brand new serial. How will Mr and Mrs Benson manage to run the guest house near Oxington? How will their children settle at school and in the village? Who is the first mysterious guest? You will meet many memorable and lovable characters including Mr and Mrs Desai, and, of course, grandpa.'

Part of scene is then shown.

Press release

You will need to tell the Press about the actors taking part.

⇨ Write something on your own including a piece on the young actors you have discovered to take the parts of the children. You often see this kind of thing in newspapers and magazines.

Acting and improvisation

We are mainly concerned with scripting soaps in this Step, but you may like to act out the scenes you have written. One way to write a scene is to improvise it first and then script it.
If you do improvisation at your school you may like to try this method in your group. You will quickly see what works and what sounds real.
You may like to tape a scene. The main problem with this is unwanted background noise you get in school. Or, if you have a video camera, you might like to see what the problems of video recording are.

⇨ It is now time to put into practice everything you have learned about soap operas. In small groups, write a full half-hour soap episode – time it by reading or acting. No scene must be longer than about a page or two. End the episode with a cliff-hanger.

ASSESSMENT

You are going to have your episode assessed by a panel of experts – one of the other groups. They are experts because they have been engaged in the same exercise as you. First you must choose a person to present and represent your episode to the panel. She or he must be clear about the aims of your piece – what you were trying to do. Prepare your representative for questioning by the panel.

1 What objections might they make?
2 How would your next episode resolve the situation at the end?
3 Have you created real characters who are different from one another?
4 Is your plot 'real' but exciting?
5 Why might an audience prefer it to an existing soap on TV?

In doing this you will have prepared questions for the representative of the group that comes to you. The representative will read through your episode with the panel; they will stop reading at any time to ask questions. When the representatives return to their groups the panels will write a report of 100–150 words on the episode they have read through.

— — — — — — — — — — — — — — — —

'Stress classes' for schoolgirls fed on a TV diet of glamour

By RICHARD CASEBY

TV SOAPS give teenagers such unrealistic expectations of a glamorous life that a girls' school has started running 'stress classes' for disappointed pupils.

Problems arise because many adolescents desire an adult life, but are too emotionally immature to cope with all its complications, say educationalists.

So fifth form pupils at the State-run Oldfield Girls' School, in Bath, Avon, are being taught how to overcome their worries with classes in stress management and relaxation led by a psychologist.

Soaps like EastEnders, Neighbours and Grange Hill show exciting lives. By comparison those of ordinary pupils can seem boring, said deputy head Vanessa Mann.

"The girls end up wanting to be seen as adults, but they don't have the maturity to cope with the demands of adulthood,' she explained.

'Certain programmes have a very bad effect. Many pupils watch them — and while some are unaffected — others think: "I've got to be like that."'

Is there life after soaps?

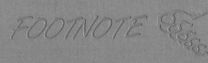

The above article was seen in the *Daily Mail* on 16 November 1988.

▭ What do you think of the last quote? Has a soap affected you in any way? Discuss this in class.

Are you becoming conscious of when you write a *verb*? Does your teacher sometimes remark that you could have picked a better verb? Do you over-use 'got', for instance? Some characters will use a wider range of verbs and vocabulary than others.
In the last footnote (page 21) you invented nouns that contained the idea of particular adjectives. But eliminating adjectives would mean the invention of thousands of new nouns. But there is a case for cutting down on *adverbs* in English – those words that assist verbs.

The case against adverbs

Can we do without adverbs?
An adverb's name tells us its job in a
sentence; it adds to the verb, telling us
when, how or *where* the action was done.
For instance, what are the adverbs in these
sentences?

1 John worked hard.
2 Jane retired yesterday.
3. I live nearby.
4 Alnaz felt sad.
5 She held him firmly.

To find the adverb you need to ask *when?*
where? or, most often, *how?* after the verb.
Are any of the above adverbs useless?
Consider the sentences without them. Are
they the same ?

Now consider this paragraph.

The bowler rushed quickly to the crease;
Tariq swiped wildly at the ball as it whizzed
rapidly towards him. The ball soared high into
the air. A fielder on the boundary plodded
slowly towards the ball, his hands held up
hopefully. The ball dropped rapidly and
lodged firmly in his hand and he laughed
happily as he threw it triumphantly into the
air.

▭ Pick out the adverbs in this piece and
then read it without them. Has the piece
been altered? Not really. Nearly all the
ideas of the adverbs are already contained
in the verbs – the action words.
Which adverbs are still necessary?

Use verbs with precise meanings

Try to use verbs that have precise
meanings. There's often a large choice.
This brings us to your *vocabulary* – don't
let it rust. Your vocabulary is the words you
know, the words you can use. Most people
limit the use of their vocabulary,
particularly in their writing.

▭ How many of these *synonyms* (words
of similar meaning) for 'walk' do you
know?

> lumber, pace, patrol, plod, prowl, ramble,
> roam, saunter, shuffle, slouch, stagger,
> stalk, stride, stroll, strut, swagger, trudge,
> waddle.

Which, for instance, would be the best to
show the movement of:

> a fat man, a tired man, a proud woman, a
> clumsy woman, a drunken man?

You could test your knowledge of these
words by demonstration – volunteers to
walk in a particular manner for the rest of
the class to guess.
How many of these words do you know
and never use? Why not?

EVERYDAY ENGLISH

3

This Step deals with the language you need for everyday living, both spoken and written.

Role play – 'Our Town'

You are the citizens of Penton, a small seaside town in Gromshire. You each need a copy of the outline (Map A on page 35) to construct your town.

Stage one

▭▷ Choose the character you are going to be in this town. Write a short paragraph about yourself and your work. Use your own name but make up the rest of the details. You may be a business person in the town, owning or working in a shop, bank, hotel, factory, etc, or you may simply live in the town and perhaps work elsewhere.

Mark on your map either your home *or* your business. Do not write your name or the name of your business. Simply make a box like this.

▭▷ Now, working as a whole class, construct your town by describing in turns the whereabouts of your house or your business. Do not look at each other's map. Work in pencil; it is easy to make mistakes. The description gets easier as more people's buildings are located. For instance, the first person might say: 'Start at the southern part of the town, take the road north, turn left at the second crossroads, then first right. My sweet shop, Tony's, is on the corner of that road on the left of the 'T' junction.'

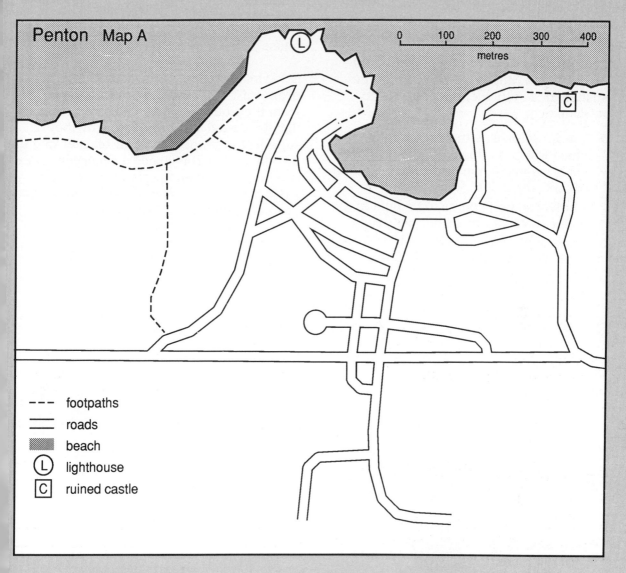

Penton Map A

footpaths
roads
beach
Ⓛ lighthouse
Ⓒ ruined castle

You would mark Tony's with a square on your map and number it 1.

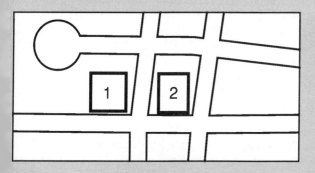

On a separate sheet of paper you will then begin the key to all the places in your town.

1 Tony's Sweets
2 Alice's Fishshop

Now build up the map. As you progress you will be able to give quicker directions. For instance, one of you might have a house or shop directly opposite Tony's. As you progress, discuss the names of your roads and write them in.

Warning: Mistakes will be made. You'll need to check your maps at the end of this stage with the rest of the class.

Stage two

Penton Town Council is considering the proposals on Map B below. Each of the shaded areas represents a proposal for development:

1. A new campsite with 200 places, 50 of which will be permanent. The proposal will bring many more visitors and about 120 new residents.
2. A hotel and golf course to be built in the northeast corner near the castle ruins.
3. A new supermarket to be built on the southern edge of town.
4. A hundred new homes.

How will they affect your business or your house? Which ones do you agree with?

⟶ Hold a meeting to discuss the proposals. You need a representative(s) from the Council to give you any further details needed and to explain why they support the proposals. (Your teacher might take this role.) You'll need a Chairperson to run the meeting and perhaps a secretary. After the meeting, discuss what happened in small groups (4–6). You might try to convert people who oppose you, or to find like-minded people who will help you plan further action – a petition, for instance. *You must stay in your role.*

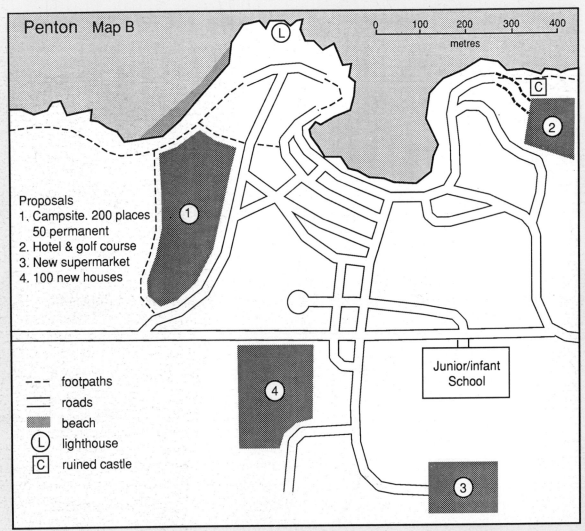

Penton   Map B

0   100   200   300   400
metres

Proposals
1. Campsite. 200 places
   50 permanent
2. Hotel & golf course
3. New supermarket
4. 100 new houses

Junior/infant School

- - - footpaths
═══ roads
▦ beach
Ⓛ lighthouse
Ⓒ ruined castle

Stage three

The Council representation now decides to show the meeting a longer-term plan for the town – for a new dual-carriageway and fly-over. Study Map C, below.

▭▷ The Council meeting is reconvened. You have to decide what you think of this new proposal. The Council representative will explain why it has been thought necessary.

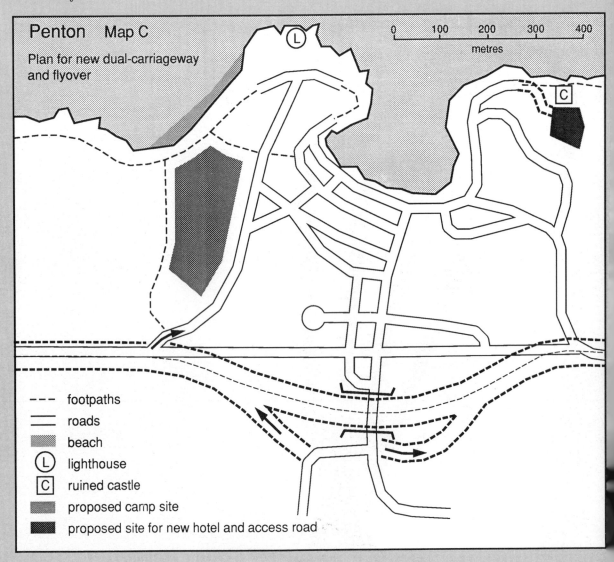

Penton Map C

Plan for new dual-carriageway and flyover

0   100   200   300   400
metres

- - - footpaths
━━━ roads
▨ beach
Ⓛ lighthouse
C ruined castle
▨ proposed camp site
■ proposed site for new hotel and access road

Further stages

1 You could prepare a plan for a new building or an extention to your house or shop. To do this properly you would need help from the Technology Department of your school. You would have to explain the purpose of your building and submit its design to the planning department (the rest or a small group of your class). There might be objections from your neighbours or other citizens. For instance, Tony might well be against the plans for another sweet shop.

2 Another meeting could discuss new amenities in the town – telephone/post boxes, street lights, traffic lights, for instance. Where should these be sited?

ASSESSMENT

Throughout this Step, you have been in rôle, expressing the thoughts and feelings of the personality you invented. Write a paragraph of 10–15 lines describing your experience. Consider these points:

1 How well did you stay in rôle? Did what you said represent the ideas of the citizen in Penton you were supposed to be?
2 How well did you contribute to the discussions and meetings?

When you have finished, swop your self-assessment with your neighbour. Does she or he agree with what you have written. Did you meet the same difficulties?

FORMS AND LETTERS

4

Much of your written English in adult life
will consist of filling in forms and writing
letters. Here we give you some practice.

Read this account of an accident.

The accident

James Allen was driving a van from Wisbech to his grocer's shop in
Sheringham one Friday morning, July 13th. The van was owned by his partner
in the grocer's shop, Graham Young, in whose name the van was insured. The
van was loaded with crates of tomatoes, sacks of apples and three bags of
carrots. As he turned a corner James saw a herd of cows approaching on his
side of the road. He braked hard and swerved right, hitting an approaching car
driven by a Mr Paul Stuart. The impact was slight, causing only superficial
damage to both vehicles. But the van, after the impact, swerved out of control
into the forecourt of a garage, knocking over a petrol pump and smashing the
plate glass as it came to a halt against the office door. The van doors flew
open and all the fruit spilt on the forecourt. James Allen sustained a broken
collar-bone; no one else was injured, but the petrol pump attendant, Winifred
Hall, was taken to hospital along with James. They were both kept in
overnight, suffering from shock. Winifred Hall witnessed the whole incident. By
the time James had extricated himself from the van, the garage forecourt was

full of cows munching fruit. The man in charge of the cows, Edwin Carson, arrived five minutes after the accident. He said he had been delayed fastening the gate of the field he had brought the cows from because the catch had been broken. Before he was taken to hospital, James exchanged addresses and names of insurance companies with Paul Stuart, who was able to continue his journey unhurt, and with only minor damage to his car.

Filling in forms

➡ Fill in the accident report on page 42–43. You will need a copy each. *Do not mark this book in any way.*
Take your time. Most people, for instance, start by getting the name of the insured wrong. You will have to invent some of the detail – telephone numbers, policy numbers, business addresses, for instance.
Make sure your plan of the accident is clear – don't include unnecessary detail. You need not draw individual cows, for instance.
It is probably best to write in pencil first. You can then rub out or write over it.

Commercial Union Assurance

Motor Accident Report

Please answer all questions on both pages as fully as possible.

Your Contact

Your Claim No.

Policyholder

Full Name   Policy No.

Occupation   Date of birth

Address

Post Code   Private Tel. No.   Business Tel. No.

Are you VAT registered? | YES/NO | What percentage can you recover? | % |

Driver

Name   Occupation   Date of birth

Address

                                  Post Code   Private Tel. No.

Is driver employed by you? | YES/NO | Was the vehicle driven with your permission? | YES/NO |

Give details of convictions for any offence (including Fixed Penalty offences) in connection with any motor vehicle:

Has the driver ever been refused motor vehicle insurance?
If YES, please give details and dates. | YES/NO |

Type of driving licence held.   Full/Provisional.   Date of first Full licence issued.

Vehicle

Make and Model   Year   cc

Reg. No.   Date of first registration

Chassis No.   Vehicle identification No. (VIN)

Owner's name and address:

Finance Company name, address and agreement no.:

Describe fully the purpose for which the vehicle was being used:

Brief description of the damage

Repairers name, address and Tel. No.:   (Mark the damaged areas with crosses)

Is the vehicle at the repairers? | YES/NO | If not, when will it be taken in?

If you are VAT registered may we authorise repairs on your behalf? | YES/NO |

If the vehicle is beyond economical repair may we move to free storage? | YES/NO |

Accident

Date _____ Time _____ am/pm Place _____

Weather _____ Visibility _____ Distance from nearside _____

What lights were lit on the vehicle? _____

Speed a) before the accident _____ mph b) at the moment of impact _____ mph

If the police attended please give a) Name of force _____ b) Officers number _____

Rough plan of Accident. Please show a) name and approximate widths of roads b) directions of vehicles

Driver's Statement (Please state fully what happened and continue on a separate sheet if necessary)

_____

_____

_____

_____

_____

_____

_____

Witnesses (Continue on a separate sheet if necessary)

Name and Address	Passenger or Independent Witness

Other Property Damaged (Continue on a separate sheet if necessary)

Name and Address	Damage (Please give Reg. No. of vehicle if applicable)	Insurer and Policy Number

Persons Injured (Continue on a separate sheet if necessary)

Name and Address	Seat belt worn YES/NO	Injury	Taken to hospital YES/NO

Declaration

I declare that these particulars are true to the best of my knowledge.

Signature _____ Date _____

Commercial Union Assurance Company plc.,
Registered in England No. 21487. Registered Office: St. Helen's, 1 Undershaft, London EC3P 3DQ

The accident – two letters

James Allen's daughter, Anna, aged eight, was staying with her grandmother, James' mother, at the time of the accident.

▭ Write the letter James might have written the following morning to Anna, telling her about the accident, and reassuring her about his injury.

James was due to play golf the following Saturday with his friend, Ali Zehar. They were to meet on the course.

▭ Write the letter James might write to Ali, calling off the game and recounting his experience.

Your letters will be different in tone. The aim of the exercise is for you to practise getting the right tone and content for a particular *audience*. Write your letters on your own and then come together in small groups to discuss how you tackled this exercise.

LIBRARY SKILLS

5

This is a group library skills project. Here is your chance to use a library as an adult might do in business.
We also take a look at the travel books and guides.

Mrs B's trip to Italy

You will need to tackle this project in groups of 5–6. Use any sources (people, books, etc) you can. *You will not be able to do the work in class.* Your school or your local library will be the best sources of information. Parents and friends might be able to help, as well as other teachers.

▷ First read the background information to the project on pages 46–47. Then each of you choose 3 to 4 questions to answer. The winning group will be the first group to complete the whole task.
At the end of the questions are some titles of books, etc. you will find useful.

Background to the project

Mrs B is planning a business trip to Italy to promote her sports equipment. After she's completed the business trip, she intends to spend a fortnight on holiday in the area. She has asked you to find out certain information for her, relating both to her work and her holiday, and to make her travel arrangements. She will be based in Rome at first. You, or in this case your group, are the secretary to Mrs B. She is the owner of Top Sports, a firm manufacturing a whole range of sports equipment.

The questions:

1 a) What is the name of the airport at which Mrs B will land?
   b) What is the distance by air between London and Rome?
   c) How long will her flight take?

2 What is the Italian currency?

3 What is today's rate of exchange with the pound?

4 Mrs B is annoying you by continually quoting something about 'When in Rome do what you like.' You're pretty sure she's actually mis-quoting this and you decide to put her right. Find the original quote and who said it.

5 Mrs B tells you that her husband is annoyed that he can't accompany her on the trip – he's always wanted to visit Rome. She's decided to buy him a present to pacify him, and has decided on a dishwasher. She's asked you to find out which is the best value-for-money machine, its price and a few details about it.

6 Mrs B has been in a bad mood for the last few days. A colleague says she's looking like Lucrezia Borgia. You don't know the reference. Find out. Should you be worried?

7 Mrs B is keen to spend part of her holiday on one of the islands near Rome. Find a map for her to see which one of these islands would suit her and find a little information about it.

8 a) She wants some books to take away with her – some science fiction books as well as some general books on Italy. Her favourite fiction author is Ursula Le Guin. Find out which books the library has by this author, and list four of them for her.
   b) Find the Dewey classification number for books about Italy – she's interested in modern history of the country as well as travel books.
   c) List three travel books with authors and titles that you think might interest her.

9 Your boss obviously cannot visit Rome without visiting the famous sights and monuments.
   List four she should not miss and where they can be found.

10 Find the names of three Italian daily newspapers that she may like to buy while she is there.

11 a) Your boss has a definite desire to visit the Leaning Tower of Pisa. The best way for her to travel is by train. Find suitable train times for a day trip, and how long the journey will take.
    b) Find some details about the Leaning Tower that you can pass on to her. Who built it? When was it built and for what, etc?

12 You suddenly remember you will need to organise a taxi to get her to the airport. Find the names and telephone numbers of three taxi services.

13 Wishing to leave no stone unturned in making your boss's holiday a success, you decide to write to the Italian Embassy in London for further tourist information. Find the address and phone number.

14 Your boss has been moaning all day about the terrible pain in her arm, convinced it is something terminal. You're sure it's only 'tennis elbow'. Find out the symptoms of this complaint so that you can convince her she's fit to travel.

15 a) Mrs B wants to take a book as a gift for her host, and has decided on *The Shell Book of Exploring Britain* by Gary Hogg. To order this you will need to find out: the name of the publisher, the price, and the ISBN, using the microfiche reader in the library.
   b) What is an ISBN?

16 Your boss is obviously getting over-excited about this trip, and you remember, thinking of her elbow as well, it would be advisable to make arrangements for medical insurance for her while she's away. Find out the form needed which is available from the DHSS, and the address of their local office.

17 Mrs B's Italian is very limited, but she feels there are one or two key words to do with her business that she has forgotten and really ought to know. Find the Italian words for the following: football, golf club, badminton, swimming pool, billiard cue.

18 Your boss's host is very keen on football, and so Mrs B is anxious to impress him with her knowledge of the 1990 World Cup. Who won? What was the score and who scored the goals?

19 This trip to Rome really has gone to her head – she's now sent you out to buy Garibaldi biscuits!
   a) Who was Garibaldi?
   b) Can you find any reference to the biscuit taking his name?

20 You feel you should reward yourself with a treat after all this hard work, with a trip to a London theatre. You fancy seeing a musical. Find out what's on at which theatre, and the phone numbers you'll need for booking tickets.

Here is a list of books in a library you will find useful:

Whittaker's Almanac
Oxford Dictionary of Quotations
Which? Guides
Oxford Companion to English Literature
Penguin Medical Encyclopedia
Chamber's Biographical Dictionary
Willings Press Guide
Daily Newspapers

It will help all your studies in school if you learn to find your way around the reference section of your (local) library.

Travel books and guides

There is a saying: 'Travel broadens the mind'. But it does only if you find out something about the country or area you are visiting. To do this there are many guide books and travel books available in libraries.

▷ Here are nine extracts from a book called *Let's Visit Yugoslavia* by Julian Popescu. On your own, decide which chapter of the book they came in. The chapters are listed after the extracts.

a) The Dalmatian coast (the name given to all but the northern part of Yugoslavia's coastline) and the offshore islands are extremely beautiful. The coast is very rocky and jagged with numerous bays and fjords. The natural scenery and the constant sunshine have made the coast popular with tourists from all over the world. There are old towns, many dating from the Middle Ages, and fishermen's villages which cater for visitors. There are wooded slopes, and terraces planted with vines, and with olive and fig-trees. There are mulberry trees, too, and groves of oranges and lemons.

b) It is usual to have folk dancing and music both at weddings and at festivals of patron saints. At wedding celebrations, the bridegroom and his bride start the dancing, which is very lively and accompanied by clapping and laughter. The festival of a patron saint is called a slava. All the people parade in the streets at these festivals. The men wear white shirts, richly embroidered waistcoats, tight-fitting black trousers and crimson pill-box hats worked with embroidery. The women wear petticoats edged with white lace, brightly-coloured aprons trimmed with gold, blouses of pure silk and bonnets with little silver bells and coloured ribbons.

c) Most of the cottages in this Serbian village are white-washed. Some are made of sun-dried bricks, called adobes. The adobes are made by hand from mud and chopped straw. The cottages have thatched roofs. There are also some houses faced with brightly painted plaster; their roofs are tiled and gable-ends are decorated. Most of the houses have a balcony or a narrow verandah, with a bench where people can sit and chat in the evenings.

d) All Yugoslav schools are free, and run by the State. Boys and girls start at elementary school when they are eight. They must stay on at school until they are sixteen, and then they may either start work or continue their studies.

e) Yugoslavia is easy to find on the map for it is the largest country in south-eastern Europe with a total area of 225,500 square kilometres (99,600 square miles). It lies on the western side of the Balkan peninsula. The word Balkan is of Turkish origin and means 'chain of mountains'. Much of Yugoslavia is covered by mountains. The population of nearly 22.5 million is made up of more than a dozen different nationalities.

f) Plums are a major fruit crop. The orchards produce sweet, reddish plums which are dried in special ovens and then exported as prunes. Yugoslavia is one of the world's leading exporters of prunes. But much of the plum crop, including windfalls and rejects from prune-making, is put to ferment in vats. The fermented pulp is distilled and turned into a strong brandy called sliv vica, the national drink of the Yugoslavs.

g) A much simpler method of transporting logs is to float them down a river. Men lash the logs together into a raft. They build a makeshift cabin on the raft, since the journey may last several days. Then these men, who have to be tough and skilled, steer the logs down the river, using huge oars to guide them past treacherous boulders and bends. At night they moor the rafts. They make a fire on the bank to cook their supper, and tell each other stories to pass the time.

h) About 2,500 years ago the plains and valleys of present day Yugoslavia were inhabited by a wild, nomadic tribe of people called Illyrians.

i) Southern Yugoslavia is much less industralised than the north of the country. There are some important mines, where valuable metals such as copper, lead chrome and zinc are extracted, but few factories. Most of the people farm plots of land or work as craftsmen in small shops or bazaars.

The chapters

1 Facts and Figures on Yugoslavia
2 Land and Climate
3 Early History
4 Industries and Resources
5 Forests and Fisheries
6 How the Country is Farmed
7 Village Life
8 Cities and Towns
9 Education
10 Sports, Entertainments and Festivals

⟹ Look at each of the chapters in 1–10 above. Decide which is useful and which is uninteresting to you and boring. What would you like to know about Yugoslavia? What kind of things do you expect in a guide book or a travel book? Would you like to know more about the language, for instance? Discuss these questions in class.

A guide to your area

▭ Write a guide to your own area. Decide, first of all, who it is for (the audience):

British people?
Foreign tourists?
Teenagers?

Remember different things interest different people. Say who your audience is in your introduction. Write about half a page on each of the chapter topics you have chosen.

The following chapter headings were listed in a travel guide to France. How many would be useful in your area? If you are writing for teenagers, are there any things missing in this list?

Getting there
Red tape and visas
Costs, money and banks
Health and insurance
Information and maps
Getting around
Sleeping
Food and drink
Communications – *post, phones and media*
Opening hours and holidays
Entertainment: *music, cinema, theatre and festivals*
Work and study
Police and thieves
Sexual and racial harassment

Your local Tourist Information Office or Town Hall will be good sources of information.

ASSESSMENT

In the same groups you used for the library skills project, decide on the best guide from your group. Think about these things when assessing:

1 Quality of information
2 Set out or lay-out of facts and information
3 Clearness of sentences
4 Personal touch
5 Unusual information provided

_ _ _ _ _ _ _ _ _ _ _ _ _ _ _ _ _

FOOTNOTE

In your guides you were trying as much as possible to help your reader. In your English code there are other things besides words which help a reader. Seen these anywhere?

" " , ' ? . ; —
: ( ) !

This looks like a particularly tricky code to crack. These little marks have a history of causing trouble to school children. Get to know them, to feel they are friends rather than enemies. Most of them have homely sounding names. One sounds like a make of van, another what the van comes to at traffic-lights and another two of the vans upside down after a crash. There's a large piece of your insides amongst them, there's half the same piece, there's a very polite swear word and a pair of the things you need to put up shelves. Finally there are marks to show the tone of voice you need for shouting and for questioning. Identify them.

Here they are in action:

'It's no good! I just can't get it right!' shouted Alan.

His teacher (he was new and not yet used to Alan's ways) came to the desk and, in a kind voice, said: 'What's the trouble, Alan? I'll go through it again, if you like.'

'Go through what?'

'The sum, of course.'

'Oh, that!' said Alan. 'I'm not bothering with that. It's just that I'm trying to draw a face on Jim's back, and he keeps moving.'

The new teacher's face reddened; he snatched the piece of chalk from Alan's hand; he marched him to the door; he opened it slowly; he shoved the boy through the door. But, despite the force of the shove, Alan did not cross the threshold, because his passage was blocked — by the Head Teacher's stomach.

52

Punctuation marks are meant to help, not to hinder, the writer and reader. They are simply *signs* to show how the writer wants his or her work to be read, so that it says exactly what he or she intended it to.

But just as we can only communicate by the use of words we all understand, so we all need to know the circumstances in which we use different punctuation marks.

A set of guidelines for punctuation

Use the passage about Alan to make a set of guidelines for using the various punctuation marks. Give an example to illustrate each one.
Compare your guidelines with your neighbour's. Who has written the clearest or given the best example?

FOOTNOTE

Here is some information that will help you understand more about a sentence and help you to punctuate one.

Agreement in the present tense

1 Those men works hard.
2 A cheetah run fast.

Doesn't sound right?
Yes, you have to change the verbs *works* and *run* to *work* and *runs* to make the sentences sound right. But you could also make them sound right by changing *Those men* to *This man* and *A cheetah* to *Cheetahs*.

In the present tense, there is a connection between the main noun (or pronoun) in a sentence and the verb.

The main noun or pronoun in a sentence is called the **subject** of a sentence. The subject of a sentence controls the verb. If a subject is plural (more than one) the verb has to be in the plural form as well. This is why *we runs* is wrong. It should be *we run* in **Standard English.**

Finding the subject

How do you find the subject of the sentence? You ask the question *Who?* or the question *What?* in front of the verb. For example:
    The girls play hockey.

The verb is *play*. You ask *Who plays*? 'The girls' is the answer; it is the subject of the sentence.

WRITING GHOST STORIES

6

Ghost stories are very popular with
teenagers. Have you ever tried writing one
of your own? Here we give you some
instruction.

What makes a good ghost story?

Read the following story:

The Old House

Janet and John walked down the road. They came to the gateway of a long
drive. There were trees down each side of the drive making it dark.

'Let's go down here,' said Janet. 'Let's explore.'

'All right,' said John.

They walked down and came to an old house. There was creeper all over it.

'I wonder if anybody lives here?' asked John.

'I'll knock on the door and see,' said Janet.

'What will you do if anybody comes?' asked John.

'I'll ask if Mr Jenkins lives here.' She knocked.

They waited. The door suddenly swung open and out came a ghost. Janet
and John ran away as fast as they could.

⮕ In pairs, discuss why this is a very badly written ghost story. Then come together as a group or class and talk about your criticisms.

Writing a good ghost story is not easy. It can be demanding to interest your readers in something unusual, frighten them a little – or a lot, and leave them thinking they have had a good read. 'The Old House' is not a well-written ghost story for these reasons:

1 It is too short. You need more details than this, if you are to entertain your readers.

2 We know nothing about Janet and John. They are not real people here. If they are scared when they go to the old house we need to know something about them, e.g. their ages, a little bit about their characters that makes them different from each other (Is one brave and the other nervous?), something about their background, perhaps something about their parents. Do they speak in *dialect*? We need to be interested in them as people for us to care about what happens to them. This is called identifying with the characters.

3 There needs to be some reason why they are near the old house. Are they on holiday? Are they lost? If they are lost, it would give us some sympathy for them. Are they looking for their dog?

4 There is a lack of description. What is the gateway like? Is it imposing or is it run-down? Is there a name to the house? Are there big iron gates to be climbed? If there are, we know they are trespassing which gives a little tension to the story.

5 The lack of description is even more apparent as they go down the drive. The good ghost story writer would make the trees creepy. They would overhang the long gravel drive making a dark tunnel. Janet and John might imagine faces in them. Branches could brush their faces. What is needed is plenty of adjectives to describe what the characters see and feel. What words could be used to make the trees dark, damp and mysterious? The writer has obviously never used a thesaurus to find a list of words he or she can use. When writing a ghost story have a thesaurus by your side. The adjectives help to build up suspense which this story lacks.

6 There is little description of the house. We really want to feel Janet and John shouldn't go near it and certainly not in it. You can do this by having vegetation growing over it, by having torn curtains in the windows with perhaps the suggestion of a white face looking out. There would be broken shutters creaking in the wind. There might be a strange noise coming from inside the house. The name of the house could suggest that something sinister is going on.

7 We mentioned the shutters creaking. But the writer has not said anything about the weather. Wind can have an unsettling effect. A thunderstorm can be very dramatic.

8 In real life, they would not go straight up and knock on the door. They might peer in the windows. The door could mysteriously open by itself and they could feel a compulsion to go in. If they did knock and an old white-faced butler shuffled to open it and when asked if Mr Jenkins was in he said: 'Yes, he is and he is waiting for you.' – then we might have an interesting story.

9. They do not explore the house. They could go from room to room. There could be cobwebs, perhaps footprints in the dust. It would fill your story full of suspense if they slowly went up creaking stairs. Here the good ghost story writer would suggest a presence of something, a feeling of intense cold, a sound or a strange light.

10 There is no description of the ghost. This is the hardest part for the ghost story writer. You have built up your readers to expect something terrifying. Are you going to let them down with a weak description. Is the ghost visible or just a voice? Is it a whole ghost or part of one like a head? Does something ooze from it? Is there a strange smell? Look at the frightening description of the ghost in the story that follows.

11 The end happens too quickly. If they just run away there is no proper ending. Are they stuck fast to the spot? Or are they chased by something? Is there a strange power over them? Do they get back home or to their holiday home safely? Does something haunt them afterwards? Or does someone like a policeman solve the mystery.

12 There are no clues spread throughout the story that something weird is going to happen. You must lay down clues and suggestions from the start that all is not well. The good ghost story writer does this to interest the reader in what will happen next.

13 The story and its title are *clichés*. This means that they are not original. On page 62 there are some ideas for ghost stories to get you started.

How many of these points did you pick up in your discussion? Did you find anything else wrong with it?

▷ On your own, improve the story 'The Old House', thinking of the points that were brought up in your discussion. Give it a new title and change the names of the children. Bring in other characters, if you wish. In fact, change it in any way you like, BUT MAKE IT FRIGHTENING!

Now read this story about an old house:

Bed but no Breakfast

John and Mark cycled down the road. They had been sent there by the warden of the youth hostel. The hostel had been full. 'Try Drum Road,' said the warden. 'There are plenty of bed and breakfast places down there.'

They were on a cycling holiday in Scotland. They had not booked at any hostel but had been lucky at getting in until this one. Now they were forced to try and find accommodation for the night and it was getting late.

The first three cottages were full and could take no more visitors. They were beginning to wonder where they would spend the night when they saw a battered notice on a broken gate-post: '. . .ed and . .kfast', it said. They could see no cottage but a track led between tall trees. A half moon was beginning to show through the top branches.

'It looks a bit creepy,' said Mark.

'Rubbish!' said John. 'Let's try it, otherwise we'll be sleeping under the stars. I'm dog-tired.'

The track wound through the trees for about two hundred yards. The trees formed a tunnel in the coming darkness. Suddenly they came upon a house. It was large and in very bad repair. Creeper grew over most of it, even the roof in places. There were shutters at the windows which creaked in the wind.

'Do you think anyone lives here?' asked Mark.

'Let's knock and see,' said John. 'It's our last chance.' He lifted the heavy metal knocker. Its sound echoed into the house. They stood listening to the rustling creeper and the creaking shutters.

'There's no one here,' said Mark. 'Let's go.'

Suddenly a light flickered through a red glass panel over the top of the door and footsteps slowly shuffled their way towards them. A bolt was shot back. The door opened.

Before them stood a man with a white beard so hairy that his face seemed all eyes. He was holding an oil lamp. 'What do you want?' he barked. The mouth was small and the beard tobacco-stained round it. He had no teeth.

'We're looking for bed and breakfast,' said John.

'You should go to the hostel.'

'It's full,' said John.

'Well, I have one room. Come in.'

The boys followed him in. The hall was full of heavy furniture covered with dust.

'Stay here. I'll get ye a lamp.' The old man shuffled off.

'We can't stay here; it's filthy,' said Mark.

'We'll just have to put up with it,' replied John. 'It's a roof.'

The old man returned. In the flickering of the oil lamp they could see that his back was bent, almost hunch-backed. 'Follow me.'

They went up a flight of stairs, the old man breathing heavily. He opened a door on the first landing. 'This is the only room I have prepared. Tak' it or leave it.'

The room was big. The wallpaper was peeling off. In one corner was a large brass bedstead.

'We'll take it,' said John.

'I'll leave you to it, then. Breakfast at eight downstairs. Oh!' the old man turned in the doorway. 'If she comes tak' no notice of her. Just tak' no notice of her.' He shut the door.

'Who's she?' asked Mark.

'Perhaps it's some other lodger,' said John, 'who's noisy, or something. Let's go to bed.'

The boys washed in cold water from a jug and then undressed for bed. The bed seemed to have more than one mattress on it and was high up from the floor.

'It's damp,' said Mark, shivering. 'God knows what my mother would say.'

'It'd be damper outside,' said John. 'It'll soon warm up. There seem to be enough blankets on it.'

'The whole house smells damp to me.' He turned on his side. 'Shall I leave the light on?'

'Why?'

'I might want to get up.'

'There's a chamber pot under the bed. I kicked it getting in.'

'Can I have the matches then?'

'Here you are.' John passed them over. He was soon asleep.

Mark could not get off to sleep. He lay, listening to John's breathing and the window shutter creaking in the wind. But he must have dropped off in the end, for he suddenly woke with a start. It was no noise that woke him but what felt like a pain in his back, as though something was digging in to him. His back was also numbed with an intense cold. At first he thought the blankets had fallen off but they were still heavy on him. The bed, with two of them in it, should have been very warm by now. Was he ill? Had he got a chill from the damp? He started to shiver. He fumbled for the matches to light the lamp but he could not find them. He lay staring up into darkness, wondering if he should wake John. An owl hooted. The shutter bumped gently on the window. Then slowly he became aware that . . . no . . . it was not possible. He held his breath. Yes . . . there seemed to be two people breathing in the room besides himself. He searched the darkness and tried, with shaking arm, to find the matches. It must be his imagination. Perhaps he had a fever. 'John!' he called. 'John!'

'What's the matter?' mumbled John.

'There's something else in this room.' As he touched John, who was further away in the bed than he thought, the intense cold went through his arm.

'Nonsense.'

'We must put the light on.'

'If you must.'

'I can't find the matches.'

'I've got another pack somewhere. Gosh it's cold in this bed, isn't it. Here you are.'

With trembling fingers Mark lit the lamp. Then he shrieked, so much that John got out of bed with him. 'Look!'

Although both boys had got out of bed, there was a depression in the pillow, as if a head was resting on it. And the blankets, instead of being flat, were all plumped up as if over a body. From the bed came a sound of snoring.

Mark opened his mouth but no further sound came.

'My God!' said John. They held each other like small children.

Then the door handle turned and the door slowly opened. The old man stood framed in the cool light of the oil lamp. 'Is she bothering you, then?' he asked.

'The bed,' stammered John.

'It's only her,' breathed the old man. 'I told you to tak' no notice. Get away with you, wifey. Away with you, you silly old hag.' The snoring stopped and the bedclothes dropped down while the pillow plumped up.

'She'll no' be back,' said the old man. 'She canna stand being spoken to harshly. You can tak' ye rest with no more worry. Goodnight.'

The two boys looked at each other. 'I could never get in that bed again,' said John.

Mark's speech had returned. 'Never mind the bed. I can't stay in this room a minute longer.'

Hurriedly, with one eye on the bed, the boys got dressed. They flung two pound notes down on the chest-of-drawers, picked up their rucksacks, crept down the stairs, unbolted the front door and pedalled hard down the track to the main road.

As the light of dawn came up they could be seen heading back in the direction of England.

⇨ Discuss the story in groups. It was written some years ago. Could minor changes be made to improve it? Discuss these points and then decide what changes you would make.

Do we need to know more about John and Mark?

Should we have more description of the house?

Is the old man well-described?

Are there enough clues to build up the suspense?

Is the climax of the ghost in the bed well-described?

Could the story end in another way? If the story was more gruesome for instance, would it spoil it?

How do you get ideas?

If you are stuck for ideas, the following suggestions should help you get started.

1 Local ghost stories are not always helpful because they lack *plot*. You need a strong plot for a ghost story. Local stories are often just about people seeing or hearing something odd.

2 But sometimes you may see a story in the local paper you can build on, e.g. a floating meat cleaver seen in the butchery department of a local supermarket.

3 Part of a ghost can be more frightening than a whole ghost. How about a story about a floating head or a hairy arm?

4 How about a ghost animal? A phantom big black dog has been seen in many parts of Britain. But how about a ghost horse or cat? Dogs are supposed to sense things humans cannot. You could write about your own dog.

5 You have heard of a ghost train, but how about a ghost car or plane? There are many ghost stories about old wartime airfields in Britain.

6 If you are really stuck look around the room you are in and play the '*What if?*' game.

   What if the view from the window suddenly changed and you saw an old-fashioned scene?

   What if you heard a mysterious voice from the television that was NOT switched on?

   What if a big lump suddenly came under the carpet and you heard a hissing?

   What if there was a sharp tap on the window and no one was there?

   What if the room was filled with a strange green light?

Now go outside:

   What if you saw someone in old-fashioned dress?

   What if you heard strange singing in children's voices?

   What if that swing started to swing by itself and there was no wind?

   What if a car came down the road and you could see through it?

▭▷ On your own, make up some *What ifs?* about a time when you were on holiday.

Write your own ghost story

▭▷ Now, using what you have learned in this Step, write your own ghost story. It would be good if they could be compiled into a class book of ghost stories and put into the school library.

ASSESSMENT

Read each of the ghost stories written by your group. Grade them in this way.
Mark A−E for:

1 Creepy atmosphere
2 Whether you could believe in them
3 Plot – a good story or one borrowed from someone else?
4 Interesting characters in the stories
5 Punctuation to help the horror, etc.

FOOTNOTE

A  report on spelling rules

It is difficult to make rules about English spelling as they don't always work in every case. Imagine you were asked to choose the 'best buys' amongst these, and to write a brief report on their usefulness.

1 Knock off the *e* for *ing*.
   make/making hope/hoping

2 English words end *ly* not *ley*.
   slowly sincerely

3 English words end *ful* not *full*.
   careful beautiful

4 *i* before *e* except after *c*.
   thief receive

5 For words ending in *y*, change the *y* to *i* before adding *er, est, es*.
   sunny/sunnier funny/ funniest
   granny/grannies

6 If a word ends in a single vowel followed by a single consonant, double the consonant before adding: *ed, est, er, ing*.
   hop/hopped big/biggest/
   run/runner stop/stopping

▭ In pairs, research the usefulness of each rule. Consider:

1 Whether the rule is easy or difficult to remember.
2 Whether you understand it.
3 How often would it be useful – think of the words you have wondered about when writing, e.g. *lonley* or *lonely*?
4 Would it just be easier to look it up in a dictionary?
5 How accurate it is – are there exceptions you can think of?

HELP!
Here is a sentence written by a student following the spelling rules:
   I won't be agreing with the proposal that my nieghbour can keep seven donkies in his field.
Which three spelling rules don't seem to apply here?

▭ Now write your report, concluding with a recommendation about spelling rules in general.

GHOSTLY POEMS AND A FUNNY PLAY

7

Nearly all tales of the supernatural and ghosts are written in prose. But here are two to enjoy in verse.
The Step will also help you in what to look for in a poem.
We also look at part of a funny radio play.

Mystery and drama

The poem you are about to read, 'Flannan Isle', is mysterious and dramatic. As you are reading, think about how the poet has achieved these affects through his:

1 presentation of the story
2 use of detail
3 choice of vocabulary
4 use of poetic effects.

Flannan Isle

Though three men dwell on Flannan Isle
To keep the lamp alight,
As we steer'd under the lee we caught
No glimmer through the night!

A passing ship at dawn had brought
The news, and quickly we set sail
To find out what strange thing might ail
The keepers of the deep-sea light.

The winter day broke blue and bright,
With glancing sun and glancing spray,
As o'er the swell our boat made way,
As gallant as a gull in flight.
But, as we neared the lonely Isle
And look'd up at the naked height,
And saw the lighthouse towering white
With blinded lantern that all night
Had never shot a spark
Of comfort through the dark,
So ghostly in the cold sunlight
It seem'd, that we were struck the while
With wonder all too dread for words.
And, as into the tiny creek
We stole, beneath the hanging crag
We saw three queer, black, ugly birds –
Too big by far, in my belief,
For guillemot or shag –
Like seamen sitting bolt-upright
Upon a half-tide reef:
But as we neared they plunged from sight
Without a sound or spurt of white,
And still too mazed to speak,
We landed and made fast the boat
And climbed the track in single file
Each wishing he was safe afloat
On any sea, however far,
So it be far from Flannan Isle:
And still we seemed to climb, and climb
As though we'd lost all count of time
And so must climb for evermore;
Yet, all too soon, we reached the door –
The black, sun-blister'd lighthouse-door
That gaped for us ajar.

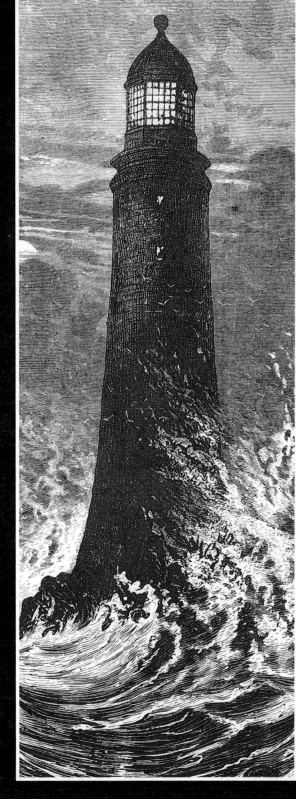

As on the threshold for a spell
We paused, we seem'd to breathe the smell
Of limewash and of tar,
Familiar as our daily breath,
As though 'twere some strange scent of
    death;
And so, yet wondering, side by side,
We stood a moment, still tongue-tied,
And each with black foreboding eyed
The door ere we should fling it wide
To leave the sunlight for the gloom:
Till, plucking courage up, at last,
Hard on each other's heels we passed
Into the living-room.

Yet as we crowded through the door
We only saw a table spread
For dinner, meat and cheese and bread,
But all untouched, and no one there:
As though, when they sat down to eat,
Ere they could even taste,
Alarm had come and they in haste
Had risen and left the bread and meat,
For at the table-head a chair
Lay tumbled on the floor.

We listened; but we only heard
The feeble cheeping of a bird
That starved upon its perch;
And, listening still, without a word
We set about our hopeless search.
We hunted high, we hunted low,
And soon ransack'd the empty house;
Then o'er the Island to and fro
We ranged, to listen and to look
In every cranny, cleft or nook
That might have hid a bird or mouse:
But, though we search'd from shore to shore
We found no sign in any place,
And soon again stood face to face
Before the gaping door,
And stole into the room once more
As frighten'd children steal.
Ay, though we hunted high and low
And hunted everywhere,

Of the three men's fate we found no trace
Of any kind in any place,
But a door ajar and an untouched meal
And an overtoppled chair.

And as we listened in the gloom
Of that forsaken living-room –
A chill clutch on our breath –
We thought how ill-chance came to all
Who kept the Flannan Light,
And how the rock had been the death
Of many a like lad –

How six had come to a sudden end
And three had gone stark mad,
And one, whom we'd all known as friend,
Had leapt from the lantern one still night
And fallen dead by the lighthouse wall –
And long we thought
On the three we sought,
And of what might yet befall.

Like curs a glance has brought to heel
We listen'd, flinching there,
And looked and looked on the untouch'd
    meal
And the overtoppled chair.

We seem'd to stand for an endless while,
Though still no word was said,
Three men alive on Flannan Isle
Who thought on three men dead.

W.W. Gibson

queer – strange
curs – dogs

Presentation

Complete this sentence as if you were one of the men who set out to investigate the lighthouse's failure.

'We suspected something awful might have happened because already . . .'

When you have written your sentence you will have begun to re-tell the story in its natural order. Why does the poet change this natural order and tell us what has happened earlier only at the end?

Detail

A ship has reported to the men that the lighthouse is not working. They are obviously an official crew, men used to the sea. They would know all the local sea birds; the limewash and tar of the ships would be familiar to them. How has the poet used this to increase the mystery and the men's fear?

The climb up to the lighthouse seems endless. But they reach the door 'all too soon'. They stand in front of it 'side by side'. They enter 'hard on each other's heels'. Explain why the poet uses these phrases.

Vocabulary

In each of these lines from the poem one word has been changed. Find the correct word and say why the poet chose it.

'With broken lantern that all night'

'We walked beneath the hanging crag'

'That stood for us ajar'

'The door ere we should push it wide'

Poetic effects: similes

Here are some *similes* from the poem:

'Like seamen sitting bolt-upright'

'As frighten'd children steal'

'Like curs a glance had brought to heel'

These are all comparisons to explain something unfamiliar by reference to the familiar. How is each *simile* helping the reader to see or feel as the men did?

Poetic effects: repetition

'And still we seemed to climb, and climb
As though we'd lost all count of time
And so must climb for evermore;'

'And looked and looked on the untouch'd meal.'

Why does the poet repeat the words *climb* and *looked*?

Poetic effects: rhythm

Notice how the **rhythm** of some lines hurries the reading on; at other times the rhythm is purposely slower. Look at these examples:

'And so, yet wondering, side by side,
We stood, a moment, still tongue-tied,'

'Hard on each other's heels we passed
Into the living-room.'

Which reads more quickly? Why would the poet want a different speed of rhythm? Find other examples.

The shortest lines nearly always occur at the end of a verse. Find examples of where a short line comes as a dramatic climax to a verse.

Here is a prose equivalent of the last two lines of the poem:

> All three of us stood thinking of the three dead men.

How has the verse form made this ending much more dramatic?

Be an investigative reporter

You hear about the disappearance of the lighthouse men and go to investigate. Write what you discover in the form of a newspaper article. You may discover a realistic explanation (but remember you have to account for a series of disappearances) or you may find something that deepens the mystery.

ASSESSMENT

In groups of 4–5, discuss each other's reports. Decide which one best explains all the mysterious detail and which one deepens the mystery in an interesting way.

— — — — — — — — — — — — — — — — — — —

Now read this poem, which was written in 1798.

Goody Blake and Harry Gill

A TRUE STORY

Oh! what's the matter? what's the matter?
What is 't that ails young Harry Gill?
That evermore his teeth they chatter,
Chatter, chatter, chatter still!
Of waistcoats Harry has no lack,
Good duffle grey, and flannel fine;
He has a blanket on his back,
And coats enough to smother nine.

In March, December, and in July,
'Tis all the same with Harry Gill;
The neighbours tell, and tell you truly,
His teeth they chatter, chatter still.
At night, at morning, and at noon,
'Tis all the same with Harry Gill;
Beneath the sun, beneath the moon,
His teeth they chatter, chatter still!

Young Harry was a lusty drover,
And who so stout of limb as he?
His cheeks were red as ruddy clover;
His voice was like the voice of three.
Old Goody Blake was old and poor;
Ill fed she was, and thinly clad;
And any man who passed her door
Might see how poor a hut she had.

All day she spun in her poor dwelling:
And then her three hours' work at night,
Alas! 'twas hardly worth the telling,
It would not pay for candle-light.
Remote from sheltered village-green,
On a hill's northern side she dwelt,
Where from sea-blasts the hawthorns lean,
And hoary dews are slow to melt.

By the same fire to boil their pottage,
Two poor old Dames, as I have known,
Will often live in one small cottage;
But she, poor Woman! housed alone.
'Twas well enough when summer came,
The long, warm, lightsome summer-day,
Then at her door the *canty* Dame
Would sit, as any linnet, gay.

But when the ice our streams did fetter,
Oh then how her old bones would shake!
You would have said, if you had met her,
'Twas a hard time for Goody Blake.

Her evenings then were dull and dead:
Sad case it was, as you may think,
For very cold to go to bed;
And then for cold not sleep a wink.

O joy for her! whene'er in winter
The winds at night had made a rout;
And scattered many a lusty splinter
And many a rotten bough about.
Yet never had she, well or sick,
As every man who knew her says,
A pile beforehand, turf or stick,
Enough to warm her for three days.

Now, when the frost was past enduring,
And made her poor old bones to ache,
Could anything be more alluring
Than an old hedge to Goody Blake?
And, now and then, it must be said,
When her old bones were cold and chill,
She left her fire, or left her bed,
To seek the hedge of Harry Gill.

Now Harry he had long suspected
This trespass of old Goody Blake;
And vowed that she should be detected –
That he on her would vengeance take.
And oft from his warm fire he'd go,
And to the fields his road would take;
And there, at night, in frost and snow,
He watched to seize old Goody Blake.

And once, behind a rick of barley,
Thus looking out did Harry stand:
The moon was full and shining clearly
And crisp with frost the stubble land.
– He hears a noise – he's all awake –
Again? – on tip-toe down the hill
He softly creeps – 'tis Goody Blake;
She's at the hedge of Harry Gill!

Right glad was he when he beheld her:
Stick after stick did Goody pull:
He stood behind a bush of elder,
Till she had filled her apron full.
When with her load she turned about,
The by-way back again to take;
He started forward, with a shout,
And sprang upon poor Goody Blake.

And fiercely by the arm he took her,
And by the arm he held her fast,
And fiercely by the arm he shook her,

And cried, "I've caught you then at last!"
Then Goody, who had nothing said,
Her bundle from her lap let fall;
And, kneeling on the sticks, she prayed
To God that is the judge of all.

She prayed, her withered hand uprearing,
While Harry held her by the arm –
'God! who art never out of hearing,
O may he never more be warm!'
The cold, cold moon above her head,
Thus on her knees did Goody pray;
Young Harry heard what she had said:
And icy cold he turned away.

He went complaining all the morrow
That he was cold and very chill:
His face was gloom, his heart was sorrow,
Alas! that day for Harry Gill!
That day he wore a riding coat,
But not a whit the warmer he:
Another was on Thursday brought,
And ere the Sabbath he had three.

'Twas all in vain, a useless matter,
And blankets were about him pinned;
Yet still his jaws and teeth they clatter,
Like a loose casement in the wind.
And Harry's flesh it fell away;
And all who see him say, 'tis plain,
That, live as long as live he may,
He never will be warm again.

No word to any man he utters,
A-bed or up, to young or old;
But ever to himself he mutters,
'Poor Harry Gill is very cold.'
A-bed or up, by night or day:
His teeth they chatter, chatter still.
Now think, ye farmers all, I pray,
Of Goody Blake and Harry Gill!

drover – person who drives (on foot) animals to market
pottage – thick vegetable soup
canty – singing
casement – window

In small groups, discuss how the poem makes use of the same techniques as 'Flannan Isle'. Consider:

1 presentation: the order in which the story is told
2 use of detail
3 choice of vocabulary
4 use of poetic effects.

How does the poet make the catching of Goody and Goody's curse dramatic?

An investigation

Read the introduction and the short play extract on page 71. Then answer the following questions.

What are the real names of these people? When and where did they live? What did they do? One of them wrote 'Goody Blake and Harry Gill'. Which one? Use the clues and the extract to find enough information in your library to write a brief **biography** (life story) of each of the characters.
A bonus for anyone who can find the true identity of De Quisling, mentioned in the extract.

What advantages can a story in verse have over a story in prose? Why were many of the stories of early man in verse? Discuss these questions in class.

Here's a short piece of script from a recent radio series called 'The Wordsmiths of Grossmere'. The main characters are:

William Wordsmith and his sister, Dotty;
Cholericke, who keeps talking about a poem called 'The Ancient Mariner';
Sheets, who has just begun writing a poem about a nightingale beginning 'My heart aches ...';

In the extract, Sheets has come from London to Grossmere to meet Cholericke and Wordsmith. Wordsmith organises a cricket match to entertain Sheets, and begins the commentary. Mary, Wordsmith's wife, is batting.

WORDSMITH	'A cricket match is being played Upon our orchard-grass: And Mary's stroke, tho' long delayed, A scorching boundary was – It passed between De Quisling's knees A space not one foot wide Cholericke gave chase, but soon was seized With pains in his inside.'
CHOLERICKE	Ah! 'Tis the Wambling Trots – I must retire, beneath the hazel bush ... You, William, must assume the role of wicket-keeper.
WILLIAM	Then you, Cholericke, must supply the commentary.
DOTTY	Cannot I supply the commentary, William?
WORDSMITH	Do not be foolish, Dotty. Throw Mr Sheets the ball.
CHOLERICKE	'Ah! Cricket is a gentle thing Beloved from Pole to Pole: To Mary's bat the praise be given She smote the ball far into heaven: In clouds it made a hole. We stood tranfix'd and open-mouthed At Mary's mighty stroke It whizzed far up, then dropped straight down Towards the roofs of Grossmere town
FX	Distant crash. Tinkle, tinkle
CHOLERICKE	And several windows broke.'
WORDSMITH	I think that concludes our game, Ladies and Gentlemen.
DOTTY	What a shame, William, but it is growing dark.
CHOLERICKE	A thick black cloud blots Phoebus from our view –
SHEETS	Well played, everyone!
FX	Distant rumble of thunder. Nightingale sings
SHEETS	Ah! My nightingale!
DOTTY	Oh! Dear Mr Sheets will be able to conclude his poem!
SHEETS	Yes, indeed: here is my pen and paper – I required only to hear once more the nightingale –

Phoebus – the sun

FINDING THE FACTS

8

The better we can read the more we can find out about the truth of things. Newspapers and magazines are a good source of facts about our modern life. We can read in them ideas about how we live today and the latest research going on. Here we ask you to look at some newspaper articles on bullying at school.

Writing an article on bullying

All of us have some experience of bullying at school; even if we were never bullies or victims ourselves we have seen it happening.
In the first part of this Step you are to write an article of your own about bullying – after you've found out the facts from studying the newspaper articles on pages 73–77.

You are looking for the answers to these questions:

1 Is there a particular type of bully?
2 Is there a particular type of victim?
3 Are girls as likely to be involved in bullying as boys?
4 Are girls and boys involved in different types of bullying?
5 Are there any particular ages when bullying is liable to be at its worst?
6 What are parents' and teachers' attitudes to bullying?

⟹ First, make notes on your own about the articles under each heading above. You could divide two pages of your exercise book or file, with three headings on each from the six questions. For example, the first page would be divided like this.

Types of Bully   Types of Victim   Girls/Boys Involvement

Make your notes under the headings as you read the articles for the second time. For instance, your first note under *Types of Bully* might be 'usually physically strong'.

When you have made your notes, write a rough draft of your article, dealing with all the questions but using *only your notes*. Try to make it *your* article, not just pieces from the newspapers copied out. Aim for about 200 words.

Before you re-draft, read the articles a third time. Have you left anything important out? Be sure to stick to 200 words. Then redraft. You are trying to make it read smoothly. It must make sense in itself, to someone who has not read the articles.

NB: It must be written in sentence form, not note form. You are not trying to include everything in the articles. You are selecting under various headings. Much of the originals will be left out.

Now read these articles (below and on pages 74–77) together with your teacher. You may like to make a list of any new words you learn and will want to use.

NEW RESEARCH has confirmed that nearly 20 per cent of children are bullied at school but only half tell their parents or teachers.

The study of 1,000 children in South Yorkshire found that 18.1 per cent of secondary school children and 17.1 per cent of middle school children said they had been bullied.

Ten per cent admitted being bullies and of these 3.9 per cent said they bullied children once a week or more often.

The findings, which were reported today to the London Conference of the British Psychological Society, show that 8 per cent of the children in secondary schools said they were bullied at least once a week, while 5.5 per cent of the middle school children said they were bullied several times a week.

Peter Smith, of the psychology department at Sheffield University, said bullied children were likely to feel lonely and less well-liked at school. He is to tell the meeting that government action is required.

"Bullying can be very serious for its victims. These children are likely to feel isolated at school and many spend their break times alone," he said yesterday.

Dr Smith will describe a Norwegian government project which has reduced bullying by half. "We hope that the Government here can be persuaded to support a similar campaign." There, bullying has been reported to be two or three times above British levels.

He said more than half of the children in the survey suffered in silence. But he said parents were within their rights to inform the police or to take legal action if attacks could be classified as assaults.

Parents who suspect bullying should encourage their children to talk about it, see if they can get support from their friends, and if necessary approach school governors about the problem.

Most bullying takes the form of teasing he found, but in a quarter of cases it was more serious and could involve attacks.

Dr Smith's work confirms the belief that one-in-five children suffer bullying during their school careers but does not support the view that the problem may be greater. Some believe that as many as 75 per cent of chilren are bullied at school.

Bullies are more often boys than girls; two thirds of those who said they were bullies also reported that they had never been reprimanded by teachers or parents.

Victims were equally likely to be boys or girls.

By Celia Hall Medical Editor

Parents can help break the grip of the bully

Geraldine Taylor examines ways in which the disturbing school phenomenon can be tackled.

MY MOST chilling insight into the nature of bullying came when, with the zeal of a probationer secondary teacher, I tried to protect the victim of it. A deputation of older (and in other respects kindly) boys assured me that my interference would do more harm than good. It was, they explained patiently, simply the victim's *turn*.

Childhood is too precious to be spent in the chill of dread, isolation and shame felt by the bullied. Few parents need convincing of this. Of the 50 parents of primary school children who discussed this with me, 38 felt bullying to be the most serious school problem their children were likely to face — or had faced already — and 14 parents were dealing with bullying at the time. One mother had even joined the school staff as a dinner lady to keep an eye on her bullied daughter.

Recent research among 1,000 Cleveland schoolchildren bears out these high figures — but parents whose children are being bullied find cold comfort in surveys, historical perspectives or debates about what is and what is not 'bullying'. The need is for immediate relief.

Believing themselves to blame, many bullied children do not turn to us for help at once. We sense something is wrong — there is a sad atmosphere, an abrupt clamming up or listless shrug if we ask about school and friends. Children may suddenly want to come home to lunch — or take a variety of routes home to avoid the bully. They may become desperate to own some object which 'all their friends' have. There may be torn clothing, bruises, scratches or, in extreme cases, children steal to meet the bully's demands.

Should we punish the school? Do we know the whole story? A child's account of bullying can be confusing and contradictory — reflecting the cat and mouse nature of the experience. Sometimes, too, parents feel ashamed. 'I couldn't admit to anyone that Pauline was bullied,' one mother told me, 'I was so ashamed she wasn't popular.' 'My dad kept repeating "Why *you*, what have *you* done",' said Michael, aged 14.

We are not powerless. We must refuse to let the problem isolate *us*. We can understand that some of the patterns of bullying are predictable and can be broken. Certainly we can mitigate the worst effects.

There is an almost ritual quality to the bullying pecking order — an element of 'turns' exists — but some children have longer 'turns' as others join in the taunts and or digs — relieved they are not on the receiving end.

The bullied child is often different in some way — smaller, shyer, a stammerer, wearing unfashionable shoes, a harder worker. Children are faced with a choice — conform if they can and be 'accepted' or hold out and be bullied. Often, though, conformity is impossible: you cannot change height. If we suspect this is the case with our children — we can help by realising how much their self-esteem and confidence is at stake — and by doing all we can to restore and boost this at home.

We must also seek the co-operation of our children's teachers. Many parents are sceptical of the school's ability to deal effectively with bullying. Two parents felt their sons' secondary schools turned a blind eye to it, believing it would toughen children up. Most schools, however, are coming to take bullying very seriously, although teachers face even more complex aspects of it — the bully who complains of being bullied, the bullies who appear highly popular and the fact that bullying rarely takes place where a teacher can see it.

I talked to the heads of 12 schools, both primary and secondary. All wanted to know if bullying was happening. Some preferred the child to be the one to tell the staff — but others believed this to be unrealistic.

Approaches to coping varied, but most heads agreed that all-round communication among the staff was the key — with all staff concerned being on the look-out for incidents and being firm when they occurred. Some schools have specific strategies to prevent bullying. Parents are informed every time their child is involved in a fight — no matter whose fault it appears to be. The staff also write the child's name in a book, which is burned at the end of the term so that the child can make a fresh start.

The message from schools is encouraging. Rather than denying the problem, they are looking for ways to combat it and believe that dialogue with parents is vital. 'Tell us,' one head urged, 'it's not just learning that is affected by worrying about bullying. It's family and school happiness. I'm not getting into a discussion of whether bullying will always be a part of childhood. I'm concerned with doing something about it *now*.'

Beating off the playground b

Hilary Wilce reports on schoolchildren who live in fear

Intimidation among pupils is not confined to public schools

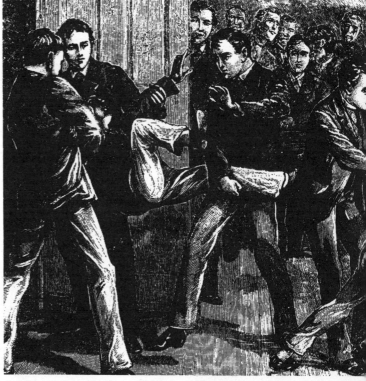

"I WAS bullied all through school. It went on for years. I was small and clever and had rather undeveloped social skills.

"Then one day it came to a head. They got me in the corner of the playground and Vicky Miller said — I can still remember the exact words — 'Let's pinch her till she cries' — and I finally went berserk. After that I refused to answer to Titch or those kinds of names. I had a friend by then, which gave me some confidence."

To this 38-year-old woman, what happened at a London independent school a quarter of a century ago is as vivid as yesterday and has left its scars. "I'm definitely a bit paranoid, and I hate people being left out of things. Did I tell my mum? No, never. Not a thing."

Bullying is as old as schooling itself, but has always been masked by the secrecy of shame and fear. Now there is mounting evidence that serious bullying is widespread, and some schools are trying new ways of tackling it.

According to a recent survey by *Mother* magazine, more than a quarter of primary school pupils are likely to be involved in bullying, and 38 out of 50 parents interviewed thought that bullying was the worst problem their children were likely to face at school.

Academic research echoes these high figures. Pete Stephenson and Dave Smith, educational psychologists working in the North-east of England, surveyed a representative sample of more than 1,000 Cleveland children in their final year of primary school and found that 23 per cent were involved in serious bullying, as either bullies or victims.

"Of course it is always difficult to define what bullying is," Pete Stephenson says. "We tended to look at cases which had been going on for longer than a year. But it can vary from a horrible case we had, where two children had urinated on a third, to milder name-calling — even though being called 'square eyes', or whatever, is terrible to the child being teased."

The most substantial investigation into bullying has been done by Professor Dan Olweus, in Norway, following the suicides of three children who had been bullied at school.

He found that boys were more likely to be involved than girls. They used physical aggression, while the girls' chosen weapons were verbal maliciousness and social manipulation. Boys bullied both boys and girls, of the same age or younger than themselves, while girls picked on girls in their own class. Olweus also discovered that, far from being the social inadequates that many imagined, bullies tended to be strong, confident and quite popular.

The research by Smith and Stephenson agrees with the finding that the majority of boy bullies are physically strong and assertive and, although unpopular with teachers, are not necessarily so with other children. However, they also found a small group of "anxious bullies", who tend to be widely disliked and to have educational problems.

Victims, too, are of different types — the kind of weak, passive and anxious children that might be expected, "provocative victims" who seem actively to seek out confrontation, and a small group of unfortunate and much-despised children who are both bullies and bullied.

Boys use physical aggression, girls social manipulation

Of course, much bullying is short-lived, and fluctuates over time. The first year of secondary school is a volatile patch, and some schools notice a resurgence in the fourth year, when pecking orders are strong. But the work of Smith and Stephenson on persistent bullying suggests that there is significantly more in larger schools and in poorer areas, and that both victims and bullies tend to be disadvantaged compared with other children.

This contrasts sharply with the popular image of bullying as the invention of the upper classes in their sadistic boarding school rituals.

A City analyst recalls being a new boy at Haileybury in the early 1960s. "There were endless punishments for things like being 'cheeky'. They included holding up Corps boots for a long time, sitting on unlit gas rings, drinking evil potions ... all condoned by the prefects. It left me totally cynical about what people are capable of." His main tormentors, he notes, are all now leading figures in their professions.

However, Geoffrey Walford, lecturer in sociology at Aston University, and the author of a book on public school life, maintains that that type of bullying is extinct. "All you get now is the normal sort of verbal bullying, no worse than anywhere else, and probably better. The problem at boarding school is that you can't get away from it at the end of the day."

New forms of bullying have replaced the old. The recent inquiry report on the murder of a 13-year-old Asian boy by a white boy at Burnage High School, Manchester, in 1986, highlighted grimly the problem of racial bullying and teachers' unions have expressed anxiety about the violence and aggression now shown by very young children.

"An awful lot of push and shove goes on in infant schools. You get bullying in the Wendy House, and it almost certainly reflects what goes on at home", says Delwyn Tattum, reader in education at the South Glamorgan Institute of Education, and currently editing a book on bullying. He says there is no way of telling whether bullying is increasing or not. "What the figures do show is that there are an awful lot of unhappy children in schools, and if they are unhappy

Teachers are anxious about violence by very young children

in school, their performanc[e] bound to be impaired." Smith[?] Stephenson argue vehem[ently] that the view of bullying as ['nor]mal" — held by many teache[rs] is totally unacceptable. "Bul[lying] is another form of abuse, [from] one child to another. It ca[uses] genuine distress to victims, a[nd] is not in best inte[rests] of the b[ully] to allow continue"[.] Pete Step[hen]son. Sc[hools] they say, can and must try to c[re]ate an ethos where bullying is [out]lawed. They should adopt [a] school-wide discipline pol[icy,] develop a good classroom a[tmo]sphere, ensure that cloakro[oms] and hidden corners are we[ll] pervised, and encourage vi[ctims]

to confide in a trustworthy adult. "One of the schools here actually has a phrase, 'We are a telling school'," says Pete Stephenson.

At Salendine Nook High School in Huddersfield, a large 11-16 comprehensive, problems of serious bullying have been successfully tackled through a mixture of pastoral care and curriculum work.

"We try and build up the victim's confidence and teach basic social skills — things like, don't try and infiltrate the group or bribe your way into it, but develop a relationship elsewhere if you can," says Graham Herbert, head of year.

The school sometimes changes the composition of classroom groups so that bullies and victims are working together, and introduces notions of bullying into English, geography, history, and economics lessons. In English, pupils might study such books as *Lord of the Flies*, and be encouraged to express their feelings through imaginative writing. Modern history might introduce the notion of larger, richer countries bullying smaller, weaker ones.

Such an approach can eradicate even an entrenched problem within a term, Graham Herbert says. He adds: "Every instance is different and demands a different answer. The main thing is that it is made explicit that the school condemns bullying in a very positive way, and it does not do it through bullying the bully, but through supporting the victim."

ASSESSMENT

Selecting information from quite different passages and making an article of your own is probably the most difficult process in the study of English. You have now been through that process. Write a paragraph of ten lines that would be useful for someone else tackling this project. Consider:

1 Is it best to make notes as you read or to read the whole passage first and then re-read looking for the points under each heading?

2 How many notes did you make? Did it turn out to be the right number when you came to make a rough draft?

3 Were your notes copied word for word from the articles or did you begin to use your own words as you made them? For example, your first note might have been 'usually physically strong' or simply 'big and strong'. Which method would you recommend?

4 Did you manage to make your article from your notes alone, or did you have to look back at the passages?

5 How many longer sentences did your final draft of 200 words contain? Many short sentences may be a sign of the 'scissors and paste' method – making a sentence for each note in the passage.

When you have written this paragraph of advice you will also have made an assessment of your article.

▭▷ Read the advice for parents below. In pairs, discuss this and decide how useful it is from your own experience.

— — — — — — — — — — — — — — —

Practical steps you can take

If your child is bullied

■ Listen calmly and question gently: who is involved, where is it happening? How long has it been going on?

■ Don't react with hand-wringing horror: your child may then feel responsible for the downfall of family happiness.

■ Agree that bullying is distressing. Explain that it happens to most children, but it is going to be sorted out and it will cease.

■ If you feel that this is more than a short flare-up of quarrelling or teasing, contact the school.

■ Don't approach the parents of the bully. They may see things in a completely different light.

If your child is a bully

■ Calmly tell your child what you have heard and listen to his/her story.

■ If there has been bullying, tell him/her it must stop at once, making it clear that it is the behaviour you dislike — not your child.

■ Is there any obvious reason for your child to be seeking extra attention?

■ Many bullies feel badly about themselves. Boost their self-confidence, focusing on their feelings and interests.

■ Show your children how much your friends mean to you — and try to discuss the value and nature of friendship.

▭ Now, on your own, make an advice column, based on these pieces and your own experience. Your column should give advice to victims, parents and teachers.

▭ Write an account of a bullying incident or series of incidents in which you have been personally involved or have witnessed.

FOOTNOTE

What punctuation marks would you use for this passage?

I looked at my watch it was five o'clock in the morning this was always a dangerous time we had the dawn at our backs the enemy would see us outlined against the sky

You could decide that there are five separate sentences and use full-stops and capital letters to indicate this. You could decide that each group of words is so short that you don't need the strongest pause – the full-stop – and use semi-colons instead. *NB:* The shortest pause, a comma, would not be right for this. There is a third alternative, not to use strong punctuation marks at all:

When I looked at my watch, it was five o'clock in the morning, which was always a dangerous time because we had the dawn at our backs and the enemy would see us outlined against the sky.

The groups of words have been linked by *conjunctions*. The most common conjunctions are:

after, although, and, as, because, but, if, since, so, than, that, though, unless, until, when, where, which, who.

Conjunctions offer you a choice. Do you agree that nothing is lost by the use of conjunctions here?

Look at these examples from the articles about bullying.

My most chilling insight into the nature of bullying came *when* I tried to protect the victim of it.

Dr Smith's work confirms the belief *that* one in five children suffer bullying during their school careers *but* does not support the view *that* the problem may be greater.

A conjunction to beware of is *and*. This is a very useful word, but do not overuse it.

▭ There are seventeen points in the following passage where you need to make a decision about whether to use a punctuation mark or a conjunction. Re-write it, making your choices. Compare your version with your neighbour's. Have you made the same decisions? Remember: there is no need to use *and* at all.

It was the summer a group of people was watching a man on a soapbox he was telling people of the rewards they would receive if they voted for his party a pensioner was in the crowd he was bent and ragged the preacher thought he would use him he would be a good illustration of his case he asked the crowd to look at the old man saying that such people would have luxury flats when his party was elected ungratefully the old man said he didn't want a luxury flat he was happy where he lived the speaker suddenly leapt from his soapbox the crowd's reaction had been hostile all through his speech this was the last straw marching up to the old man he seized him by the lapel shook him until his teeth rattled 'you'll do as you're told if we put you in a luxury flat you'll stay there'.

YOUNG POET'S CORNER

9

In this step we would like you to judge some poems written by young people.

The poems on pages 80–83 were chosen from over 41,000 entries to the *Observer* newspaper's National Children's Poetry Competition. Most were written by children of your age.

▭ In groups of 4–5 read them through and judge them for yourselves. Decide which one you would award first prize.

Judging poetry

Judging poetry is difficult, sometimes as hard as deciding whether a screwdriver is better than a saw. It depends what you want it for. The most important thing to decide is its purpose, what it is trying to tell the reader. So in each case you're not comparing like with like. You are deciding how good the saw, how good the screwdriver. Does the poet achieve his or her purpose, make you feel and understand as he or she felt? Comment on the choice of words, the use of rhythm,

rhyme, similes, metaphors (see below) – the whole way the poem is presented. But these are only useful aids to the poet's purpose; they have no value in themselves.

▭ When you have made your comments and decisions as a group, write an individual report on your findings, reflecting the whole group's feelings, not just your own.

FOOTNOTE

A **metaphor** is a word or phrase or sentence used to describe something which is not literally true.

> Mum ironed out my problems.

Ironed is a metaphor because, strictly speaking, only an iron can iron.

> The moon slunk beneath a cloud as if ashamed to show its face.

This whole sentence is a metaphor. Can you give three reasons why? Look at *slunk, ashamed* and *face*.

Cherry

The first of many goats to come,
Her coat a wiry gloss brown,
Ears flopped beside her head
And huge pleading eyes of a hazel colour.
Her Roman nose making her look
   superior. . .
The mouth that was always chewing
And was passed down to her kids
Who could undo shoe laces, pull buttons off.
Her most outstanding feature was her head,
Constantly butting people playfully.
It was like the waves bumping against a boat.
She was tough and obstinate,
A bully amongst our growing herd.
When milking time came, she would stand, a
   statue,
Occasionally looking round to check
   everything was all right.
Then the day came when she fell ill.

She walked around, dejectedly,
A solemn face, set, hard as a stone.
Gradually weaker every day,
No longer the bully of the herd
But a meek and feeble lamb.
She didn't even attempt to butt,
Just lay, a victim of illness.
It got too bad, too painful for her and us to
   bear.
We had to call the knackers.
It was for her own good.
The men came with their gun.
They weren't even going to take her away
To do the work of the devil.
I ran, trying to escape her weak face.
Bang!
I cried all of that day.

Naomi Raven

I Remember the Day

I remember the day my friend had to go.
A big blue removal van pulled up outside his
    house.
There was a lot of confusion,
Shouting, talking.
His mum was directing a man
Carrying their best table,
A well-built, tattooed man.
He was whistling to a man at an upstairs
    window
And shouting something about a bed.

But my friend was nowhere to be seen.

I was standing by the gate,
Leaning up against the lamp-post,
Seeing how far I could kick pieces of stone.
I looked up
And saw one of the removal men
Bolting the back of the truck.
The truck started up,
Leaving a cloud of dust as it sped off.

Through the dust, I saw
The go-kart we had built together,
Left against their fence.
I slowly walked home,
Pulling it behind me.

Jon Allen

Brave Soldiers

He was five when he died
My brother.
The wall collapsed
Burying him prematurely.
He left a wreath of red fingers
Poking from the rubble.
They shaved his hair to look at his
    brains.
They pulled a face from the bloody
    mess.
They put a time bomb in his chest
And cruelly dragged him back to life.
Paul was only five and we
Don't speak of him any more.
Lying beneath
Thin white sheets
Concrete plaster flesh and wires
All wrapped up in crisp pyjamas,
He started to move
And the nurses beamed
One fraction of finger
Twitching life into him
After months of rigor mortis.
Never speaking or smiling
He waited passively till death
Choked him on tea one morning
And he forgot how to cough,
Went blue and escaped
Across the wires, over the plastic
    joints
Running, a brave little soldier
Fighting our cowardice
His artificial breath.
Searching the screen for a trace
They told us he had deserted.

Elizabeth Macfarlane
(Beacon in Cornwall)

Last Respects

When Duggan's came to
take him away there
was no room for me and
so I sat on the
floor where all I could
see were black legs in

black trousers under tweedy
overcoats and black
stockings with best shoes
that didn't fit properly
because they were kept for
times like this which

are always expected but
never anticipated. All the
people he used to
know had come to see
him, reminiscing, and
he had missed Them.

Then They all went out to see him to
pay their last
respects but I don't think it
was him in there because it didn't
look like him. He was
fatter and I was alone

until They all flooded back
in and I knew that it was time because
there was nowhere else to go.

I was all in knots and my body
ached because there was
no room, and because the last time
I saw my grandad he was
confined to a
coffin.

Joanne Holroyd

Mourne

Mourne country. Under
    Chimney Rock,
they cut the granite
    block by block.

Mourne country. When
    a neighbour dies
he chops the mountains
    down to size.

Mourne country. Half a
    parish sent
its contours for a
    monument.

Mourne country. On the
    broken bones
we pile the hills for
    symbol stones.

Mourne country. Daily,
    chink by chink,
the tombs rise and the
    mountains sink.

Mourne country. Will
    we soldier on
till all our Commedaghs
    are gone?

Mourne country. We
    have graves to make.
How many Binnians
    will it take?

Kerry Carson (Belfast)

NB: Tombstones are
made in Mourne.
Binnian and Commedagh
are hills.

Friend!

He'd brought me
Through the kitchen
And up the stairs
To show me his friend.

I imagined
Another person like him –
Shy and slightly embarrassed.
But that's not what I found.
I didn't find anything.
Well – nothing that fitted the description
    'friend'.

The bedroom
Wasn't what you could call tidy.
I glanced round the room
And looked at Albert.
Smiling he went
To a white cupboard set into the wall,
Out of it he took
. . . A stuffed squirrel!

I looked at Albert again.
He was looking at it
With an affectionate look on his face.

I turned green.
How could his friend be a stuffed squirrel?
A thing that doesn't move –
Just stares.
If that's a friend,
I don't want one.

Rachel Brown

FOOTNOTE

'A little learning is a dangerous thing.'

This quotation is certainly true for using the **apostrophe** to show ownership. A little learning about the apostrophe can make your writing worse.

Most people can manage to use the apostrophe to show a letter or letters missing – *can't, haven't, doesn't,* etc. But not many people can use the apostrophe to show ownership accurately. Which group are you going to join?

The main point to remember is illustrated by the notices above (all of which are wrong!) – you don't need an apostrophe every time you see an s. These three rules will work every time. But you must make sure you use them correctly.

When to use

1 The apostrophe is needed for the owner, not what he or she owns.

  Mary's books   Girls' coats
  The sun's rays

Where to use

2 If the s on the end of the owner is needed to show a plural, the apostrophe goes on the outside. Remember this by *SPO*:
  S – Plural – Outside.

Make an effort to understand this rule. Look at these examples.

  children's books   ladies' hats
  horses' hooves   donkeys' tails
  a miner's lamp   that cat's owner
  the barber's shop   women's shops

The first and last examples are the tricky ones. The s on the end of *children's* and *women's* are not needed to show plurals. *Women* and *children* are plurals without the s – so the apostrophe goes inside.

When not to use

3 Apostrophes are not needed on pronouns.

  yours   ours   theirs   its

NB: *It's* with an apostrophe means *it is*. The apostrophe is to show the *i* has been missed out. It is not to show possession.

Help with apostrophes

▷ Test your neighbour on the three things you have learned in this footnote. Then let him or her test you. If you do not agree on the answer consult your teacher. Look for examples of twenty uses of the apostrophe for ownership used in this book. If you do not understand them, consult your teacher.

Make a special effort to use them correctly in your own work. *There is no short cut, no easy way to learn apostrophes. If there were, we wouldn't see examples of their misuse every day.*

MYTHS

10

In this Step we want you to look at a folk tale. People have always loved a good story. We all like our imaginations stirred, it seems. Children, in particular, love a magical tale.

An interesting thing about myths, folk tales and legends is how much truth there is in them as they tell about the early times of the people of this planet. Is there any basis for the Cyclops, for instance? Could there, at any time, have been one-eyed giants?

Myths, legends and folk tales

Myths, legends and folk tales are a treasured part of tellings and writings that have been handed down to us by past generations. Many are so old that it is difficult to trace where they originally came from.

Myths, legends and folk tales are often concerned with the following:

1 attempts to explain *how* things happened or *why* things happened, e.g. the creation of the earth and its wonders.
2 tales of the great heroes and heroines, the wars they fought and the deeds they did, often on great journeys.
3 great crimes.
4 great disasters.

The mystery that surrounds them is part of their charm. Was there a King Arthur? Did Beowulf slay Grendel?

Read 'The Gift of the White Cockatoo', a folk tale from Papua, New Guinea.

The Gift of the White Cockatoo

A long time ago, when the world was young and new, there were still some people who had not discovered the existence of fire. They used to shiver when the weather grew cold, and all the food they ate was raw and uncooked. They had no fires in their villages where they could sit and gossip and tell stories; in the hours of darkness, only the moon gave them light.

In one such village, close by the sea, there lived a beautiful girl called Dawe. The young men of the village had eyes only for her. They looked with admiration and desire upon her smooth, dark skin and shining eyes, and ignored all the other girls. This made the other women jealous, so jealous that they plotted to get rid of Dawe. 'Then the young men will look at us instead!' they told each other. 'They will see that we, too, are young and comely!'

Every year, at a certain time, all the young women used to paddle their canoes across the sea to the island that stood farthest away from the mainland. This was the season for gathering seashells, which the villagers used for different purposes: as eating and drinking vessels and for decoration. The most rare and valuable shells of all they used as money. The price of a bride could be calculated in shell money, and a sorcerer would accept a certain amount of shells to make a spell or avert evil. Happy the man who wore many precious shells around his neck at the dancing ceremonies!

As soon as the young women beached their canoes upon the shore of the islands this year, they scattered to pick up all the shells they could find, placing them carefully in the bilums, the string bags they had brought with them. A few of the most precious shells were to be found at the bottom of the sea, and some of the girls dived through the gently rolling surf to fetch them up.

Dawe felt tired after the long journey from the mainland. When she had drawn up her canoe on to the sand, she lay down under a palm-tree to rest. The hot sun made her drowsy, and soon she was fast asleep. As soon as the other girls saw she was asleep, they quietly got into their canoes and paddled away, taking Dawe's canoe with them. They had planned to do this before they left the village; by going to sleep, Dawe had made it easier for them to carry out their plan. Half-way between the island and the mainland, the women sank Dawe's canoe, then paddled back to the village happy in the thought that now, without Dawe, the young men would look at them with admiration and desire.

Beneath the swaying palm-tree on the island, Dawe still slept. Suddenly a coconut husk fell upon her; she woke with a start. She looked around. How quiet it was! She could not hear any laughter or chattering — there was no sign of her companions. She went to the place where she had left her canoe and saw that it had gone, along with all the others. She saw all the footprints leading into the water, and knew then that the other girls had deserted her.

She began to weep, but above the sound of her weeping she heard a voice calling to her from the palm-tree. She looked up and saw a white cockatoo.

'Your companions have left you alone on the island because they were jealous of you,' the Cockatoo told her. 'They have gone back to the village, where they will say that your canoe overturned and sank, and that you were drowned. So no one will come to look for you.'

When Dawe heard this, she wept more bitterly than before, but the Cockatoo told her to dry her tears. He promised to look after her until her people returned to the island in a year's time, when the shell-collecting season came round again.

'Will you fetch food for me?' Dawe asked.

The Cockatoo nodded his handsome, crested head, and Dawe told him to fly to the village and bring all the taro that was growing in her garden. So the Cockatoo flew back and forth across the sea many times until he had brought every plant from the garden.

'Now we can eat,' Dawe said, and she took up some of the raw taro and offered it to the Cockatoo.

'What!' he exclaimed. 'Do you eat taro like that? Raw? You should cook it first!'

'Cook?' asked Dawe, puzzled. 'What is that? My people always eat their food just as they find it.'

Then the Cockatoo took two dry sticks and began to twirl them around each other, so that they rubbed together. In a little while a spiral of smoke appeared, and finally they burst into flame. When Dawe saw fire for the first time, she leapt back in alarm.

'What is that heat you have made?' she asked fearfully. 'Are you a magician? Have you stolen the sun?'

The Cockatoo told her not to be afraid. 'This heat is called fire,' he said. 'More and more people are learning its use. When men have fire, they no longer feel cold; they are able to make light in the darkness; and they can cook their food.'

He showed Dawe how to cook the taro on the fire, and when it was ready, they ate it together.

'How sweet and good the taro tastes when it is cooked!' Dawe exclaimed. 'How I wish I could show all the people of my village this fire, so that they too could cook their food, and make warmth and light!'

A year went by. Dawe made a new garden on the island, and lived there happily with the white Cockatoo. Sometimes, however, she thought sadly of the family she had left behind in the village, of her father and mother, her brothers and sisters. And now the season for collecting shells came round again, and once more the young girls of the village prepared to come to the island. By this time, everyone believed that Dawe had died, even the girls themselves; they did not think she could have survived alone on the island.

Many of them had become wives during the year, and they no longer felt neglected and unhappy.

'This time we will go with you to the island,' the young men said. 'No other girl must drown as Dawe did. We will make sure this does not happen.' And when they spoke Dawe's name, their eyes were sad as they recalled her beauty.

Imagine everyone's astonishment when they got to the island and saw Dawe standing on the shore, waiting to greet them.

'What happened? How is it you are still alive? We thought you had drowned!' the young men exclaimed.

The young women were silent and fearful, but Dawe did not reveal how they had deserted her, for she did not want the men to turn against their wives.

When the young men and women saw the fire Dawe had made on the island, they drew back fearfully, just as Dawe herself had done when she first saw the bright flames.

'Is this truly Dawe, or is it her ghost?' they muttered. 'Surely this is strong magic.'

Dawe told them how the Cockatoo had revealed the secret of fire to her, and taught her how useful it was. And when they all went back to the village, they lit the first fire there, and began to cook their food, to warm themselves, and to lighten the darkness with torches. And always after that they made sure that their fire never went out.

Dawe's family were proud that their daughter had shown the people the use of fire. Gladly they agreed that she might become the wife of the white Cockatoo, and their marriage feast was celebrated with glad rejoicing.

▭ In small groups, discuss the following:

1 What did you think of this as a story? Is it still a good story today? Would it make a good cartoon film, for instance? Do any parts of the story seem ridiculous today?
2 What does this folk tale try to explain?
3 From the story, what things do we learn about this primitive society?
4 Do you think this story was invented to answer a child's question: 'Where does fire come from?' or is there more to it than this?
5 What do you think is the most interesting part of this folk tale?
6 Why do animals and birds (including monster ones) play an important part in tales of early times? (Big white birds were regarded as magical in several cultures.)
7 In the myths and legends you have read, how are men and women portrayed? Are the heroes usually male, for instance?
8 Do you know a myth which you think is based on truth?

Role play

▭ Imagine you are the islanders of this folk tale. One of you recount from memory the story that you have just read. You can put in bits of your own detail.

▭ One of you tell a story in response to a child's question: 'Why does the moon shine?' (the moon could be a god or a person) or 'Why are there fish in the sea?'.

Myths and legends today

Today we often try to explain things by using scientific or historical facts. But there are still unexplained mysteries and our love for stories is so strong that legends are created all the time.

Is there a mystery about the Bermuda Triangle? Are there such things as flying saucers? Is there a yeti? Which pop groups have become legend? Is there any mystery about any of them? Which sporting heroes and heroines of our times will become legends? Who is the most famous person in Britain today? Will he or she become part of a legend?

Inventing a story

⟹After discussion in your group, invent a myth to explain one of the following:

1 the Loch Ness Monster
2 flying saucers
3 why we might be the only people in our galaxy
4 why we polluted the earth.

Write your myth down for the other groups to read or tell it to them.

FOOTNOTE

Look at these spelling strategies.

How do you spell *beginning*?
s t a r t

What about *possess*?
o w n

And *immediately*?
a t   o n c e

Perhaps not so much a strategy as a trick. But one of several worth considering, if you are one of the unfortunate people for whom the spelling of some words is a continual *nuisance* (spelt t r o u b l e).

Most people can spell 90 per cent of the words they usually use. It's the other 10 per cent that they continually get wrong. Those 10 per cent aren't hard to find. The list opposite, for instance, is used by most people. It is our choice of the most commonly mis-spelt words.

Try them on yourself – and on members of the adult world who say children can't spell nowadays. In fact, you can spell much better than people of your age thirty years ago.

Here are strategies for remembering some of these words.

1 The main one is to cover up the word you can't spell and then write it out. Repeat until you can do it.
2 If you can spell *bus* you'll never mis-spell *business*.
3 Write *appoint* and *appear* first and then add *dis* in front.
4 Remember *cess-pit* and you'll get ne*cess*ary right.
5 'Double everything' will help you remember the most commonly mis-spelt word of all – *accommodate* – 2 Cs, 2 As, 2 Os, 2 Ms.
6 Remember the town *Ely* and you'll spell sincer*ely*, extrem*ely*, fortunat*ely*, etc, quite fre*ely*.

⟹ Work out some strategies of your own. *Rhythm* is difficult to spell. Any suggestions?

Put the list into alphabetical order in your Spell Well book. Group any words that you think could go together, e.g. disappoint, disappear.

List of common spelling errors

exaggerate
character
a lot (two words)
usually
address
amount
possess
receive
probably
opinion
beneath
biscuits
broken
ceiling
clothes
colour
despite
decide
description
disgusting
does
doesn't
dropped
etc.
themselves
choose
committee
libraries
whose
successful

foreign
competition
appearance
any
accommodate
minute
opposite
disappear
solemn
agreeable
development
separate
height
procession
occurred
league
nuisance
believe
finally
disappoint
behaviour
argument
business
necessary
beautiful
professional
guard
sincerely
until
friend

anything
beneath
someone
really
seize
occasion
occasionally
meant (*no apostrophe*)
learnt (*no apostrophe*)
interest
in case (two words)
idea
preferred
immediately
humorous
coming
heard
having
happened
frightened
flies
everyone
everybody
surprised
beginning
descend
parliament
cigarette
neither
programme (*not the computer one*)

MAKE YOUR OWN PLAY

11

Here is a family play to read. We then ask you to make your own play or scene. We give some advice on the subject and an assessment procedure.

A play about a family

While you are reading the following play, think about what makes it seem true to life.

A Model Pupil

Cast:

Jane
Mr Jones
Mrs Jones
Miss Heaven
Samantha
Narma

SCENE ONE – Jane's house

JANE (Looking at newspaper) Look, be a top model for a small fee. It says so here.

MR JONES You're not going to go on about that again, are you?

JANE I'm not going on about anything. But look, they're starting a top model agency here in Brudford.

MR JONES Who says it's a top model agency?

JANE It says so here, Dad.

MR JONES Take what you see in a newspaper and divide it by a half.

MRS JONES You know how keen Jane is on being a model.

MR JONES And you know how keen I am on her doing well at school.

You can't do well at school if you fill your head with that nonsense.

MRS JONES	She's always said she wanted to be a model since she was tiny.
MR JONES	I wanted to be an engine driver and I ended up laying bricks.
MRS JONES	All the more reason to let her explore her dreams.
MR JONES	And who pays for her dreams?
JANE	It says: 'Small fee'.
MR JONES	What's small?
JANE	At least I could go along and see.
MRS JONES	We have a little saved up.
MR JONES	That's for Blackpool.
JANE	I could get a job delivering papers.
MR JONES	I'm not having that. You'll be half asleep at school.
MRS JONES	You are a killjoy, Dad. Everything she suggests you put down.
MR JONES	If there's one thing I've learned in life it's common sense, lass. There's lots of opportunities for those with the education I never had. She's bright and I'm not having her ruin her school career by filling her head full of modelling nonsense.
JANE	(Running out in tears) You just don't understand!

SCENE TWO – Next day

MRS JONES	I've got him to agree.
JANE	Oh, Mum.
MRS JONES	But he says he wants to come with you.
JANE	Oh, Mum. I don't want him there. Anyway, he's working.
MRS JONES	He'll take half a day off, he said.
JANE	He'll put the damper on it.
MRS JONES	I'll be there as well. I can handle him. You know his bark's worse than his bite.
JANE	Oh, Mum, this could be the start of something big.
MRS JONES	I know you'll make a model. I wish I could have been one.
JANE	I'll do it all for you, Mum. You'll see.

SCENE THREE – The Ajax Modelling Agency

MISS HEAVEN	Do come in Mr and Mrs Jones and Jane. Take a seat.
MRS JONES	Thank you.
MISS HEAVEN	So you want to be a model, Jane.
JANE	Yes.
MISS HEAVEN	What sort of model?
JANE	A catwalk model.
MISS HEAVEN	Yes, you've come to the right place for that.
JANE	Do you think I have a chance?
MISS HEAVEN	Just walk up and down.

	(Jane does so)
	Right, tilt your head to one side. Now the other. Take longer steps. Put your left hand on your hip. Right. Yes, I think we can do something for you.
MR JONES	Only think?
MRS JONES	Dad!
MISS HEAVEN	You can never be certain in this business, Mr Jones. But I've a good deal of experience and I should say Jane has what it takes.
JANE	Oh, good.
MISS HEAVEN	She will need to take our course.
MR JONES	She's still at school.
MISS HEAVEN	I realise that from her form. We would just do it at the week-ends.
MR JONES	What would it cost?
MISS HEAVEN	It's £120.
MR JONES	That's a bit steep.
MRS JONES	Dad! If you think it's worth it, Miss Heaven.
MISS HEAVEN	I do.
MR JONES	Is that all the cost?
MISS HEAVEN	No, then there's her portfolio.
MR JONES	Portfolio?
MISS HEAVEN	That's a wallet of photographs we send to clients wanting models, dress designers, shops, TV etc.
MRS JONES	Oh, TV.
MR JONES	And what does that cost?
MISS HEAVEN	Two hundred pounds.
MR JONES	Two hundred pounds!
MISS HEAVEN	I only engage the best photographers of West End quality to show off our models, Mr Jones.
MR JONES	I've got some photos of her, good ones.
JANE	(Embarrassed) Dad.
MISS HEAVEN	Snaps are no good. I must have real professional work or she won't stand a chance.
MRS JONES	Like those photos in *Vogue*.
MISS HEAVEN	That's right.
MRS JONES	You always have to pay for quality, Dad. You've said so yourself.
MR JONES	Still two hundred pounds on top of the other. That's our Blackpool money gone.
JANE	(Squirming) Dad.
MRS JONES	I'd love her to be a model, Miss Heaven.
MR JONES	Oh, all right.
MISS HEAVEN	You won't regret this when she's earning big money.
MR JONES	What do you mean by big money?
MISS HEAVEN	Well, you can get a thousand pounds a day on some assignments.
MRS JONES	Just think of our Jane earning that!

SCENE FOUR – At school two weeks later

SAMANTHA	What do you do there, Jane?
NARMA	Yes, do tell us.
JANE	Well, I walk up and down on this catwalk.
SAMANTHA	How?
JANE	(Demonstrating) You have to walk like this with long strides but looking natural.
NARMA	(Imitating Jane) I could do that. Watch. (Narma and Samantha laugh and walk up and down. Jane is a bit put out)
SAMANTHA	What else do you do?
JANE	Miss Heaven talks a lot about make-up and things.
NARMA	When are you going to get a job?
JANE	Not until I leave school, she says. But she's going to send my portfolio off when it arrives.
SAMANTHA	I wish I was you. What an exciting career.
NARMA	Me too.

SCENE FIVE – Jane's house

JANE	(With wallet) Look, Dad, my portfolio!
MR JONES	(Examining it) A portfolio? It's just four misty photographs.
JANE	That's the modern style of photography.
MR JONES	I paid two hundred pounds for those.
JANE	Miss Heaven's sending them out.
MR JONES	What a rip-off. How's this course going?
JANE	It finished last Saturday.
MR JONES	Four Saturdays for £120 quid?
JANE	Yes.

MR JONES	I'm going to that agency to ask for a refund.
JANE	Dad, don't embarrass me. They said I've done so well I don't need any more lessons. They gave me a diploma. Look.
MR JONES	What good's that?
JANE	It says I'm qualified as a model. Miss Heaven says as soon as I'm sixteen to let her know.

SCENE SIX – Jane's house two weeks later

MR JONES	So we've been conned.
MRS JONES	I'm sorry.
MR JONES	It's no use saying you are sorry. You egged her on.
MRS JONES	Well, I . . .
MR JONES	I should have written to these people before. Found out a bit about it. Good job I saw it in the paper or we might have shelled out more. Look, the Modelling Information Service. 'All catwalk models must be at least 5 feet 7 inches in height.' Jane's 5 feet 4 inches and she's stopped growing.
MRS JONES	I know.
MR JONES	And there's more. 'Under the 1973 Employment Agencies Act an agent is legally bound to give a written statement detailing service and proposed charge and receipt.' We got neither.
MRS JONES	Oh.
MR JONES	And there's more. 'Reputable agencies never charge for courses and they pay for the portfolio shots.' We've been really conned.
MRS JONES	Who's going to tell Jane?
MR JONES	You're going to tell her. You egged her into this.
MRS JONES	Poor soul. All her dreams.
MR JONES	Now perhaps she'll get on with her education and plan for a proper job.
MRS JONES	Five feet four.

▭ After a class discussion on the play, write one of these scenes.

1 The scene where Mrs Jones tells Jane she cannot be a catwalk model because of her height.
2 The scene where Samantha and Narma ask Jane why she is so miserable.
3 The scene where Mr Jones goes to the agency to ask for his money back. Miss Heaven refuses saying Jane could still grow.
4 The scene where Mr and Mrs Jones lie in bed hearing Jane crying in the next room.
5 The scene where a drama teacher counsels Jane about other jobs that involve a bit of glamour.

Writing family plays – advice

Try to make your family play realistic. You have only a short time to develop the characters. What do you know about the Jones family? How are you *shown* what types of people they are?

Looking at dialect

One way you can add interest to your
characters is to give them a local dialect.
But use only the one familiar to you; it is
very difficult to represent someone else's
dialect. Read: 'A Collier's Wife'.

A collier's wife

Somebody's knocking at the door
  Mother, come down and see.
– I's think it's nobbut a beggar,
  Say, I'm busy.

It's not a beggar, mother, – hark
  How hard he knocks . . .
– Eh, tha'rt a mard-'arsed kid,
  'E'll gi'e thee socks!

Shout an' ax what 'e wants,
  I canna come down.
– 'E says 'Is it Arthur Holliday's?'
  Say 'Yes,' tha clown.

'E says, 'Tell your mother as 'er mester's
  Got hurt i' th' pit.'
What – oh my sirs, 'e never says that,
  That's niver it.

Come out o' the way an' let me see,
  Eh, there's no peace!
An' stop thy scraightin', childt,
  Do shut thy face.

'Your mester's 'ad an accident,
  An' they're ta'ein 'im i' th' ambulance
To Nottingham,' – Eh dear o'me
  If 'e's not a man for mischance!

Wheers he hurt this time, lad?
  – I dunna know,
They on'y towd me it wor bad –
  It would be so!

Eh, what a man! – an' that cobbly road,
  They'll jolt him a'most to death,
I'm sure he's in for some trouble
  Nigh every time he takes breath.

Out o' my way, childt – dear o' me, wheer
  Have I put his clean stockings and shirt;
Goodness knows if they'll be able
  To take off his pit dirt.

An' what a moan he'll make – there niver
  Was such a man for a fuss
If anything ailed him – at any rate
  I shan't have him to nuss.

I do hope it's not very bad!
  Eh, what a shame it seems
As some should ha'e hardly a smite o'
  trouble
  An' others has reams.

It's a shame as 'e should be knocked about
  Like this, I'm sure it is!
He's had twenty accidents, if he's had one;
  Owt bad, an' it's his.

There's one thing, we'll have peace for a
  bit,
  Thank Heaven for a peaceful house;
An' there's compensation, sin' it's accident,
  An' club money – I nedn't grouse.
An'a fork an' a spoon he'll want, an' what
  else;
  I s'll never catch that train –
What a traipse it is if a man gets hurt –
  I s'd think he'll get right again.

D.H. Lawrence

Notice the difference between *accent* and *dialect*. Which of these words represent accent and which are genuine Nottinghamshire dialect words?

nobbut   mard-'arsed   socks
niver   scraightin'   mester

▭ These are from the first six verses. Find other examples of both accent and dialect.

▭ Write ten lines about the character of the Collier's Wife. What are her fears? What does she think of her husband? What advantages are there in her husband being in hospital?

▭ In small groups, discuss the following. How does accent and dialect make the character and the poem as a whole more interesting? Does dialect and accent help certain soap operas?

▭ Now write your own family play. Have a good row in your play. If the family agrees all the time there is no drama. Think about the conflict in soap operas.

ASSESSMENT

Read your neighbour's play.

1 Are the characters real?
2 Do they speak like real people?
3 Can you picture the family?
4 Can you picture the house and surrounding area where the play takes place?
5 Would you want to 'fast-forward' at any points?
6 Would you switch off at any point, if it was on TV?

Your assessment of your neighbour's play will consist of a TV criticism written for a newspaper or magazine in about 100 words.

— — — — — — — — — — — — —

FINDING THE RIGHT WORDS

12

In this step we want you to look at a newspaper article about lying and to invent a quiz.
We are also asking you to think about the right words to use again.
We then show you how to have some fun with words – remember, if you like words you are more likely to be good at English.
Finally we take a look at idioms.

Talking point

You just open your mouth and, oops, there goes another fib.

Read the article on page 100 with your teacher.

ALTHOUGH acquainted with the seven deadly sins, I'm particularly good at the one that's usually forgotten. The one I like to call the eighth sin. The one no one tells the truth about.

Lies. When do they start? Sometimes on waking. This morning I answered the phone. The caller said: "Did I wake you?" "No, no — I was just getting up." So I'd already told two lies before I'd even got out of bed.

There should be some statistic about how many the average person tells in one day. I'd modestly estimate 25.

Most people agree that lying is wrong, but it's all a question of degree. I was once given a bit of good advice: tell one lie only, but make it a good one. Somehow one is never enough.

I have to offer several to cover myself as each lie opens up a cavernous gap of fictions which needs to be filled by yet more lying.

I've always lied. The more I aim for the truth — and I do — the more I end up lying. Before I can turn around, one realise I've let another one go. For example . .

"How old are you?" "Thirty-two." (A lie.)

"What do you think about so-and-so?" "Marvellous. I've always admired their work." (A lie.)

"Do you play chess?" "Yes." (A lie.)

Why do I lie? Because these are nosey questions and I'm ashamed of the truth. So I lie. It hurts no one — it might even make people happier.

My motto is: if people are nosey, then lie to them. But then one lies for so many different reasons. Here is a true story about lying out of kindness:-

After rehearsing a spot on the French and Saunders show I was having a cup of tea when Mavis Nicholson came in. As most people do when they come into a room full of strangers, she looked round for someone friendly to talk to and found me. "Ah yes," she said. "I think I spoke to you on the phone." Even though I knew she hadn't I found myself panicking and agreed that, yes, we had talked on the phone. It was clear Mavis had mistaken me for someone else.

I was once a social worker. I wasn't the best social worker that ever lived and I suspect some of the people around me may well have picked up on this, leading to a general state of anxiety on my part. One day people were idly chatting about birthday presents. I found myself saying I was off to buy one for a friend — to get out of the office so that I didn't have to spend the lunch hour eating sandwiches and discussing work; and secondly to show that I did have a friend, someone who liked me.

I went out, saw a glass bowl in a shop, thought nothing about it and returned to work empty-handed. They asked me what I had bought and before I knew it I had lied. "I bought her a glass bowl," I said. "Oh, let's see it then," they cried. I panicked. "Oh, it's . . . er, in the car."

I rushed from the office, ran back to the shop, bought the bowl, ran back to the office and, still puffing, managed to say: "This is the bowl I bought." By this time, everyone had lost interest and barely looked up.

Why had I gone through torment, expense and stress? Because I couldn't keep my mouth shut. Sometimes people just open their mouths and lies pop out with unforeseen consequences.

An example of an elaborate sort of lie was when I was 12. I had a Cindy doll and was obsessed with getting all her outfits but my funds didn't stretch that far. I solved this by shoplifting.

My mother began to notice how Cindy was changing her outfit at least three times a day. Finally she questioned me. "Well," I said, "Captain at the Guides has asked me to sew extra uniforms for orphan guides." I said I was being paid for it. My mother didn't look convinced, which is why I had to say: "And don't tell Christine at No. 27 because she's not involved in the sewing. It's all a secret and Christine isn't supposed to know I'm doing this."

People often ask me how I manage to combine a career, a happy and fulfilled social life with being an innovative and tireless human being. Why do people ask me this? Because I lie to them.

● *Coping With Helen Lederer, by Helen Lederer, is published by Angus and Robertson (£3.95).*

Make up a quiz

✏️ On your own, make up a quiz suitable for a magazine. The quiz is entitled:

'How big a liar are you?'

Here are examples of the types of questions you might use.

1 Your best friend asks you if you like her/his new hairstyle – and you think it is awful! Do you:

   a) Smile and say it's lovely?
   b) Say it's OK?
   c) Say it really does something for her/him? (Without adding that it does something horrible!)
   d) Tell her/him that it looks vile?

2 Your Mum or Dad tells you you have to visit an uncle on Saturday – you can't stand him. Do you:
   a) Say it will be nice to see him again?
   b) Become 'ill' on Saturday?
   c) Say you must get your schoolwork done for Monday?
   d) Tell Mum you can't stand your uncle and you are going out?

Award points on the 'lying scale' for each answer. Invent a variety of situations – where would you lie and let others suffer the consequences? Would you lie to teachers, or parents in certain situations or circumstances?

✏️ Do each other's quizzes.

✏️ Discuss the circumstances where a lie or lies might be necessary. Try to make a set of guidelines

Fun with words

Read this poem.

★★★★★★★★★★★★★★★★★★★★★★★★★★

Joan
Got her ear-ring caught in the phone.
It ripped off the ear to the bone.
Which has made her rather prone
To be stone
Deaf.
Except for an intermittant high-pitched buzz
Which resounds round the cavity where the ear once wuzz.

★★★★★★★★★★★★★★★★★★★★★★★★★★

We all know that *wuzz* is a mis-spelling of 'was'. Why would it not work as well if the poet wrote 'was'?

Many people mis-spell for a purpose such as to advertise or make people take notice. This was seen on a truck:
   Wekankarryit

There is a newspaper cartoon called:
   Krazy Kat

Have you seen any cafes or other shops with mis-spellings in their names such as:
   Lite Bite?

Or have you read any poems with lines like this:
   Animals make their own strange noises
   (Far more strange than girls' or boyses')

In this extract from a poem all the funny words are really Scottish place names.

what do you do?

we foindle and fungle, we bonkle and meigle and maxpoffle. we scotstarvit, armit, wormit, and even whifflet. we play at crosstobs, leuchars, gorbals, and finfan. we scavig, and there's aye a bit of tilquhilly. if it's wet, treshnish and mishnish.

Here are three poems by Spike Milligan, a master player with words, to enjoy:

Werkling

I've werkled and werkled
The long werkling day.
I werkled and werkled
And rickled me gay.
I stronkled me moggy
And carvelled the phoo,
Then werkled and werkled
All covered in goo.
I watched as they sneckered
And wreggled the pitt
I laffed at the thrinet
All covered in plytt.
I saw forty grotties
That rood as they groked
Me know itchy trousers
That fonged when they poked.
All this I then willtressed
All this I dang sewed,
Yet not for a fackel
Took note of the sawed.
Oh no, not I gronik!
Oh no, not I will!
Oh no, nineteen wiccles!
This side of the hill!

List the words Spike has made up. Do any of them remind you of other words? Why might it be easier to make up words if you already know lots of the words in the dictionary?

Esquimau

Esquimau, esquimau
Up to everywhere in snau!
On your little sledge you gau,
Leaping from ice flau to flau.
Now I knau, I knau, I knau
Why progress in the snau is slau!

A B

A Bee!
A Bee!!
Is after me!!!
And that is why
I flee!!!!
I flee!!!!!
This bee
This bee
Appears to be
Very very
ANG
-ER
-REE!!!!!

Revision of adjectives

Remind yourself what adjectives are again by drawing some like this:

⇨ Make up your own funny poem using what you have just learned: mis-spellings, invented words, drawings of words.

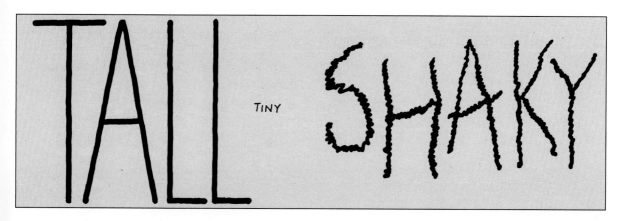

Idioms

An *idiom* is a phrase which means something different from the meaning of the separate words. For instance, to *have a square meal* does not mean something you put in the microwave in a square container; it means a good, satisfying meal.

Many of the idioms used in English have their origin way back in the past. The *square meal* comes from using a square tray or plate on board the old sailing ships. Many idioms come from sea travel. Can you think of one?

Idioms help to make English the rich language it is and the more you know the better.

Most dictionaries contain idioms. The *square meal* could be found under the word *square*, but it could also be under any of the main words of the idiom.

▭ Look up these idioms and put each in a sentence:

> let off steam
> cast pearls before swine
> make hay while the sun shines
> give a dog a bad name
> safe as houses
> play gooseberry
> eat humble pie
> on an even keel
> steal the scene
> pie in the sky

▭ Find an idiom that has one of these words in it:

> nut
> nail
> light
> lesson
> cake

Too much of a good thing

Cat? Dog? Fish? Eggs? Book?

What could all this be about? Has the writer swallowed a dictionary of idioms?

When Sammy let the cat out of the bag I had to decide whether to let sleeping dogs lie or to try and pour oil on troubled waters. One thing was for sure; I did not want to back the wrong horse by insisting that Erica was right only to find the tables had been turned. Sammy had got cold feet about it as sure as eggs is eggs. The trouble with Erica was that she would count her chickens before they were hatched. She'd only seen Ted once and she's fallen head over heels in love with him. I told her that there were other fish in the sea but she could only see him through rose-coloured glasses. All his faults — and he was a chip off the old block — were a closed book to her. It would have been a real turn-up for the book, if he had played the game and told her the truth.

▭ Discuss the following:

1 Who would invent idioms in the first place?
2 Is there a difference between a cliché and an idiom?
3 Would you be more likely to use an idiom in speech or in writing?
4 Would you say idioms make English an easy language to learn for a foreigner?

▭ Invent an idiom using something modern, e.g. a computer, a car:

> idiom: your VDU needs re-wiring
> meaning: your brain is all muddled

KEEPING DIARIES

13

Many people keep diaries. They are very valuable, if you want to become a writer. As a source of history there is nothing better because they not only tell you what happened in the past but how the people involved felt.

A historical record

If you have any ambitions to become a writer the best thing you can do is to keep a diary. The best writing by many writers is about their early lives and a diary is a wonderful aid to the memory.

It will also be treasured by your own children being partly about you and partly a historical record of your times. What you regard as ordinary now will be fascinating to people in one hundred years time.

Here are some of the things you can record in a diary:

1 What happened during an ordinary day at home and at school.
2 What happened on a special day like a birthday or family wedding.
3 Your feelings and emotions on an ordinary or special day.
4 A record of machinery commonly used.
5 The weather – particularly severe weather.
6 Illnesses and their treatment.
7 Snippets of conversation with people.
8 What you and others wore.

Here is Francis Kilvert, a clergyman who kept a diary between 1870 and 1879, writing about an illness:

Friday 18th November 1870
Went into the Tump to see young Meredith who has had his jaw locked for six months, a legacy of mumps. He has been to Hereford Infirmary where they kept him two months, gave him chloroform and wrenched his jaws open gradually by screw lever. But they could not do him any good.

How would your account of a dental filling
be looked at in one hundred years' time?

Here is Kilvert again writing about the weather.

Monday 8th July 1872
Reports coming in all day of the mischief done by yesterday's flood. Pigs, sheep, calves swept away from meadow and cot and carried down the river with hundreds of tons of hay, timber, hurdles and, it is said, furniture. The roads swept bare to the very rock. Culverts choked and blown up, turnips washed out of the ground on the hillsides, down into the orchards and turnpike roads. Four inches of mud in the Rhydspence Inn on the Welsh side of the border, the Sun, Lower Cabalva House flooded again and the carpets out to dry. Pastures covered with grit and gravel and rendered useless and dangerous for cattle till after the next heavy rain.

Discuss any storms you have been in,
particularly wind and thunder storms.

And here is his account of a dance:

Tuesday, 7th January 1873
At 8 o'clock Fanny, Dora and I went to a jolly party at Sir John Awdry's at Notton House. Almost everybody in the neighbourhood was there. There had been a children's party with a Christmas Tree at 5 o'clock, but when we drove up the harp and fiddles were going.
I danced a Lancers with Harriet Awdry of Draycot Rectory, a quadrille with Sissy Awdry of Seagry Village, a Lancers with Louise Awdry of Draycot Rectory, a Lancers with Mary Rooke of the Ivy and Sir Roger with dear little Francie Rooke of the Ivy How bright and pretty she looked, so merry, happy and full of fun. It was a grand Sir Roger. I have never danced such a one. The room was quite full, two sets and such long lines, but the crush was all the more fun. 'Here,' said Francie Rooke to me quietly, with a wild merrie sparkle in her eye, and her face brilliant with excitement 'let us go into the other set.' There was more fun going on there, Eliza Stiles had just fallen prostrate. There were screams of laughter and the dance was growing quite wild There was a struggle for the corners and everyone wanted to be at the top. In a few minutes all order was lost, and everyone was dancing wildly and promiscuously with whoever came to hand. The dance grew wilder and wilder. 'The pipers loud and louder blew, the dancers quick and quicker flew.' Madder and madder screamed the flying fiddle bows. Sir Roger became a wild romp till the fiddles suddenly stopped dead and there was a scream of laughter. Oh, it was such fun and Francie Rooke was brilliant When shall I have another such partner as Francie Rooke?
An excellent supper and we got home about one o'clock on a fine moonlit night.

Sir Roger, the Lancers and the quadrille are dances. Discuss the differences between a disco and the Sir Roger. Can you decide why this account is so lively? Why is Kilvert a good diarist?

⇨ On your own, write an account of the last disco or party you attended. Strive to get the atmosphere describing both sound and colour. How much did you dance? With whom? Record snatches of conversation with friends as Kilvert has done.

⇨ Each keep a diary for a week. Then bring in parts you want to show other members of the group. (There may be parts that are too intimate that you do not want to show.) Discuss who has given the best picture of living in the 1990s.

Log books

Log books are very similar to diaries but are normally kept by an institution. Schools keep log books. Here is one for a rural school in Suffolk.

1890

April 23rd. Field work, gathering stones, cow-keeping and farmwork has reduced the average. 35 out of 61 attended. It is impossible, in my opinion, to teach either Geography or Grammar owing to bad attendances caused by the farmers sending the children out on the fields. Many children are always ill with coughs and colds and stay at home half the year.

1901

... Alice Tilney, being 13, left school on Monday to go into service. Charles Deering was caned (four stripes) for repeated disobedience and the Brown brothers were caned (one stripe each) for stealing apples. All the big boys were caned on Wednesday for throwing stones at men working in the opposite field. John Marriage was expelled (November) for refusing to obey me. But he apologised the next morning, so I allowed him to come to school again. I administered corporal punishment to William Brown (December) for insubordination.

1928

Diphtheria has broken out in the village.
A picture 'Youth' for hanging on the wall has been received from the East Suffolk Education Committee.
The Inspector called and watched Drawing, Needlework, Singing and Country Dancing.
Two children have died from diphtheria, and Dr Stocks has taken swabs from all scholars. The school has been closed. The water-supply has been tested and it has been suggested that the children bring their own cups in future, instead of using the one enamel mug by the tap.
On Armistice Day the scholars 'listened in' to the Cenotaph Service by the kindness of Mr Bulmer, who lent them his portable wireless set.
Mary Ruth Bridge has been appointed Pupil-Teacher at a salary of £10 the first year, £12 the second year and £20 the third year. She is 15 years of age.
55 children on the Register.

---

from *Akenfield* by Ronald Blythe (Penguin)

⇨ In small groups, discuss what we can learn about school life from these short extracts from a log book. What might a teacher put in a school log book today? What would you like recorded for people to read in the future?

FOOTNOTE

It is quite common to leave out *I* in a diary.

Went to London. instead of *I went to London.*

You can also write some of it in note form:

Dentist Friday. Drill really hurt.

WRITE YOUR OWN NEWSPAPER

14

In this final Step we want you to make a study of the daily newspaper and, as a group, to write your own school newspaper. You may be asked to do this as part of your assessment as you have reached the end of Key Stage 3.

The making of a newspaper

In this Step you are asked to do some assignments as a study of daily newspapers and then, in groups, to make your own school newspaper.

Your aim is to attract as many readers as possible. You will do this by the variety of interests you cater for. You will need to consider having:

Front page articles
An editorial
A sports page
A letters page
An interview (with a local personality)
Things to do (in your area)
A fashion guide
A story
A competition page
Articles of interest, e.g. fishing, hiking.

You may be able to think of others for yourself. Each item will have a particular *style*, aimed at the particular *audience*. For instance, football and fashion pages have their own language.

You will need to consider layout and presentation, not only headlines and sub-headings, but illustrations (if possible, photographs) and perhaps some work typed or produced on a word-processor. Your school may have desk top publishing facilities but it doesn't matter, if it doesn't.

The skills you will need are to be able to:

1 punctuate in sentences most of the time.
2 write in short paragraphs.
3 punctuate quotes.
4 check spellings.
5 use capital letters correctly
6 design the layout of a page
7 research material in a library etc.
8 use different types of language to suit your readers.

⇒ You will need to work in small groups of 4–5 and the project will take about 3–4 weeks, much of the work done out of school.

But before you begin your own newspaper, work through these assignments and get into the habit of reading at least one newspaper daily.

The front page (1)

This is where the main news of the last twenty-four hours appears in a newspaper. It has big, eye-catching headlines. Look at several newspapers for the same day and discuss the news:

1 Have the papers chosen the same news to lead with?
2 If so, how do their headlines differ?
3 If so, are their reports the same or do they differ in fact?
4 Do you know where the news has come from? A reporter? A News Agency? The Government?
5 If their news on the front page differs, which piece of news do you think is the most important, the story you would have chosen, if you were publishing a paper?
6 Are there any items of news you do not think warrant being on the front page?
7 If you were buying your paper from a stand, which headline would attract you to buy the paper? (Ignore the paper your parents buy in this decision.)
8 Look at the first page inside the paper. Would you have put any of this news on the front page?

▭ Work in groups of four or five, planning the front page.
You have only space for three of the following items of news allowing for big headlines and a photo. Decide which three of the five you will include. Then plan the layout of the front page and write the headlines.

1 A new wonder drug has been claimed to have been invented by Professor Z. Isaacs of Harley University in Toronto, Canada. Just one tablet will put people off smoking for life. They will just not be able to stand the smell of tobacco in their noses.

The professor is also working on a drug for people with drink problems: 'Alcohol will turn them green after one of my tablets and they will be sick if they just sip an alcoholic drink.'

A spokesman for the tobacco industries dismissed his claims as rubbish. 'We will not stop making cigarettes,' he said, 'in fact we are increasing production as more people are smoking.'

The Health Minister, asked if he would force chronic smokers to take the tablet, said: 'It is not this Government's policy to force people to do anything.'

2 Greenearth, the environmental organisation, reports that nowhere on the planet are the oceans clean anymore. Even in the Antarctic, oil, chemicals, and plastic bottles are being washed up on the ice floes.

It predicts that there will be no fishing in a few years because the fish, if they are still alive, will not be fit to eat. Samples of fish caught show many to be dying of disease caused by chemicals.

This will lead to a serious world food shortage. Many island people rely on fishing as a major industry.

'As for swimming in the sea, it may become something you just read about in history books,' said a spokesman.

3 A new plane is being planned in America which will make Concorde look like an old bi-plane.

The new plane will fly at three times the speed of sound says a news agency report.

Details are being kept highly secret but it is believed it is due to a new metal being invented and a new jet engine that runs on water.

It would seat 1,000 passengers and be the world's biggest plane. A trip from London to Australia would take just seven hours.

4 The Government is very worried about a lack of new entrants coming into the teaching profession. 'Graduates are not being attracted into teaching because they can earn more money elsewhere,' said John Nohope, President of the National Association of Teachers. 'In science and technology there is a thirty percent shortage of teachers.'

'The National Curriculum in many subjects will just not be taught,' said Miss Joan Evans, headmistress of Raven's Park Comprehensive, Cheam. 'I am four teachers short this term. The GCSE candidates are worried they will not have the teaching to pass the exam in some subjects.'

Childen spoken to by this paper did not seem to be worried. 'We should come to school in the mornings only,' said one. 'Let's have longer holidays,' said others.

But questions are being put to the Education Secretary in Parliament this afternoon.

5 Three houses were burned down yesterday on an estate at Bradlington, Yorks.

Firemen saved the lives of twelve people trapped in the bedrooms of the houses. They were all treated in hospital for smoke inhalation and burns. Ten were detained. One baby is in a critical condition.

Chief Fire Officer Richard Hoskins said: 'It was one of the worst blazes we have had in this town on a housing estate. The people we saved are lucky to be alive because the fire station was only a quarter of a mile from the blaze. We managed to prevent the fire from spreading to other houses in the block.'

Hero of the night was Mr Jim Speechley, a neighbour, who, putting a wet handkerchief to his mouth, dashed in to save the baby.

The fire is believed to have been started by a cat, the family pet of the Williams family at No 4 Kibson Close, playing with a box of matches.

⊂⊃ Each member of the group should now start searching for school and local news that could go on the front page of their own newspaper.

The front page (2)

The front page is the last page to be completed on a newspaper before printing takes place, as late news coming in can change the layout.

⊂⊃Work in groups of four or five. Two additional pieces of news have come in. Will you need to change the layout of the paper you designed in the last assignment? Discuss this and make any changes you decide on.

A vast mysterious hole has appeared in the middle of Lincolnshire between Boston and Grantham. It is about a mile wide and its depth is unknown. It followed an earthquake recorded in Nottingham at 5 on the Richter Scale.

First reports suggest that no villages are in the affected area, but there must be loss of human life from farmhouses and cottages and from any cars that were on country roads swallowed by the hole.

Police are urging people to keep away to aid rescue services and because of the danger of further landslips.

A Japanese mini-submarine claims to have filmed the Loch Ness monster. It was filmed at the bottom of the loch using specially designed cameras and lighting.

'It is fantastic,' say the sub-mariners. 'It is about thirty-five feet long with a long neck of another twenty feet. It is covered in big white spots and was sitting on huge eggs.'

'We are now looking for more monsters in another part of the loch.'

⊂⊃Now decide which of your own pieces of news will go in your paper.

The language of advertising

The advertising copywriter works as skilfully as any poet to use language which will attract you to the product. He or she will certainly know all about a thesaurus. As you look through newspapers and pick out adverts, you will see words and terms like:

low in cholesterol;   smooth; dazzling white;   country-tasting; wholesome;   energy-packed; designer made;   comfort; ozone friendly.

▭In groups of four or five, look at the language of these three adverts and note down what you think are the important words or terms and anything else that might make the consumer want to buy the product:

2 SMOOTHPRESS

Do you know anybody who likes ironing? WE DO!

They are the owners of Smoothpress, the ironing robot of the next century.

Type into the computer the garment and material and Hey Presto! the robot does the rest.

What's more your clothes come out smelling of a choice of six natural fragrances.

Creases or pleats no problem. Nothing is a problem to Smoothpress.

No more backaches or ironing blues.

Trade in your old iron now.

1 THE AMBER

This is the ultimate small car that feels like a big saloon.

Room for five even with the long legs of our lovely model.

Yet as nippy as a motor-bike with a staggering 70 miles to the gallon.

Built round a stainless steel strengthened cage for safety.

Nothing to rust on a scratchproof body shell.

Rush round to your dealer now for a test drive.

You will be amazed at the deal he has to offer.

Then get ready to go!

3 THE MERLIN

The Merlin Computer – technology so advanced we hardly know how it works ourselves.

Answers any question you want to know about schoolwork in any subject up to GCSE standard.

No more low grades.

A must for your sons and daughters. A must for you as well. No longer will you feel ignorant about modern teaching methods.

Advises on the dreaded coursework.

Based on 3,000 books.

Printer available.

Easy to use.

Only £1,000!

⇨ Using some of the techniques used in the three adverts, draft your own advert. Each member of the group is to produce a draft and then pool your ideas for a final advert:

1 Advertise a potato as if it was a newly discovered vegetable.
2 Advertise a toothpaste that makes teeth a fluorescent white or colour of choice.
3 Advertise a funny book.
4 Advertise a new chocolate bar that tastes of Coke.

Now look through the adverts you picked from the papers again. Do you still think the one you picked as the best, is the best? What do you think about the language it uses?
Go through several more in the papers and underline what you think are key words or terms used to sell the products.

⇨ Now make your own adverts for things you could sell in a school shop. You could also include in your paper any advert done in this assignment.

The sports pages

Many people turn to the sports pages first in a newspaper. They want to know about their favourite team or sporting personality or just to get up-to-date with the sporting news. The back of the paper often has big headlines on sport just as the front page highlights important news.

⇨ On your own, read some of the sporting news from a paper. Make a list of the sports covered, e.g. football, basketball, etc.

1 Are there any sports that are not covered? You may be a fan of street hockey, for instance. Remember some sports are seasonal.

2 As you got used to the language of advertising, become familiar with the language used by the sports writer. He or she will want to make the sport or a personality sound exciting.

3 Decide on what you think is the best piece of reporting. Did it make you want to be there? Could you picture it from the words used ? Were any essential things you wanted to know missing? What would you want to know about one of these: a football cup match; a tennis match at Wimbledon; a race at the Olympics; a school match of any kind in your local paper; a snooker competition; a darts match?

4 In the paper you have probably read news that was not about an actual match or event but about people or other things: a row (argument); a personality (say a football manager); a new rule; a ban; a sponsor, etc. Make a list.

⇨ In groups of four or five, Read the following sports report:

A crowd of 23,000 packed into High Road Stadium last night. Most had gone to see giant-killers Littleton United.

The kick-off was delayed ten minutes to allow the crowd in, which helped to stoke up the tension of those already inside. It was a sea of green with Littleton supporters far outnumbering the few red hats and scarves.

Littleton went on to the attack from the kick-off. A long pass by Edwards from the centre circle found Paul Terry running free on the right and just onside. His cross to the head of his brother Jeff, who nodded it past keeper Foxwood as the defence stood around like statues, was brilliant.

Stung by this Bigton immediately put on the pressure and spent the rest of the first half in the Littleton half. But they could find no way of getting past a lion-hearted defence in which keeper Wilson was outstanding. Even a dog running in front of the goal as Ewood shot did not disturb his concentration.

The second half was even more furious with Littleton breaking the stranglehold only occasionally. Ewood hit both posts and the bar but it was as though someone had put up a sheet of steel in front of the Littleton goal. Wilson once tipped over a fierce Ramsey pile driver with his left heel.

Then to the shock of the Bigton fans, Littleton used the identical move for Jeff Terry to score again.

Fans ran onto the pitch and there was a five minute hold-up.

Bigton bombarded the Littleton goal for the final ten minutes but Wilson by now must have thought he could have walked on water. One fingertip save from an Ewood rocket was the best I have seen all season.

In the end the ref had to signal that the match was finished because his whistle could not be heard amid the roar of the Littleton fans.

⟶ On your own:

1 Write a fuller account of the match making up the names of the players after discussing as a group the language used by the reporter. How does he or she make it sound exciting? What kinds of words are used? What parts of the match does he or she focus on?

2 You can only have half the space. Shorten it after discussion as to what can be left out.

3 Make up headlines for both your reports.

Jane Scarlet, a schoolgirl, surprised more senior athletes last night at Casford Stadium when she won the ladies 800 metres. She lagged behind the rest of the field for the first 200 metres.

Mary Dace had set off at a fast pace and the rest of the field went with her, except Jane.

At the bell she was still ten metres behind and we all assumed she was out of her class.

Then came an astonishing burst which took her from first to last in fifty metres.

Amazingly she was still accelerating at the tape which she reached in 1 min. 59.4 seconds, a junior record.

Her potential as an athlete must be enormous.

▭ As with the first sports report, make a longer and a shorter version of this account. In the longer one put in an interview with Jane beginning: A hardly breathless Jane said, '...
Make up headlines for both.

▭ Now go back and read some more reports from the papers you have. Make a list of sporting terms you find and look up any you do not know in a dictionary or ask your teacher if you can't find them, e.g. volley, birdie, handicap, etc.
Then look at the photos. Are any of them any good? Is there any point in having photos in the age of TV? Do they make the layout of the page look good?

▭ Now start collecting your own school sports news. Also collect local sports news. If you have a sports personality in the area try and get an interview – remember to work out the questions you will ask beforehand.

Bias

If you strongly support one side, it is difficult not to be biased. Reporting should be fair but it is not always so in local or national newspapers.

▭ Rewrite your own report of the Bigton versus Littleton match as if you were a Bigton supporter under the headline: 'Bigton Robbed!' Blame these things for your defeat:

The pitch
The referee and his wrong decisions including not giving two penalties to Bigton
Cheating by Littleton supporters invading this pitch

▭ Your group should meet to decide whether your paper will have a bias, e.g. anti-adult; anti-pollution; anti-cruel sports; a political bias, etc.

Give him the chop

WHEN it comes to double standards, it would be difficult to match the carnivorous John Selwyn Gummer, Minister of Agriculture, Fisheries but hardly of Food.

Yesterday in Brussels, forced to face up to mounting consumer concern throughout Europe about mad cow disease, he agreed to tighter controls on the safety of British beef.

But only of beef for **EXPORT**. The new rules won't apply at home.

What is good for the French, Germans and Italians is too good for British families.

The deal should help our exporting farmers. But it won't quell any fears at home and put a beef joint back on the table of all those who can afford it. Or help farmers who rely on the home market.

Liability

And it means that British consumers are going to be made to buy and eat meat from BSE farms which could be dangerous. **THIS IS UNACCEPTABLE.**

Mr Gummer hailed the agreement as a good deal, but he shouldn't be surprised that millions of Mirror readers don't share his enthusiasm. Six months ago, he said the same controls were unworkable.

It isn't controls which are unworkable, it is Mr Gummer. He has gone beyond a joke and become a liability.

And it is time he should go.

But that isn't enough. What Britain needs, and what the Daily Mirror has repeatedly demanded, is a Minister of Food with sense and guts whose only duty is to fight for consumers.

So the Mirror today calls on them to say No to the Government's appalling compromise.

And not to buy British beef until they are given the same deal Mr Gummer has given the French, the Germans and the Italians.

Only way to beat the IRA

THIS year we are marking the 50th anniversary of our deliverance from defeat by Nazi Germany.

It was weakness towards Hitler, an attempt at appeasement, which placed us in peril.

Yet today we have Government Ministers seeking to appease evil men in Ireland.

Ulster Secretary Peter Brooke is even praised for making progress in preliminary talks with the Irish Government.

What progress? What are talks with Dublin ever going to achieve? Irish premier Charles Haughey and his accomplices will **NEVER** be satisfied until Ulster is handed over to them.

And the Protestant majority in Ulster will **NEVER** agree to rule from Dublin.

Encourages

Both Britain and Ireland condemn the violence of the IRA.

But the Irish Government encourages terrorism by identifying itself with the killers' aims.

And the British Government encourages them with every concession.

There is only one way to beat the IRA.

Prove to them that however much they maim and kill, they will not achieve their political aims in a million years.

Britain should make Ulster part of the United Kingdom, like Scotland and Wales, like Cornwall and Northumbria.

In the end, the IRA—and even Dublin—will get the message.

Task for T-men

THE police are to set up a nationwide intelligence unit.

That is good news.

The bad news is that a national police service like the FBI in America is being ruled out.

This is a pity.

Terrorists and other violent criminals are better organised than they have ever been.

Their evil reaches beyond national frontiers.

Society must deploy all its resources to fight them.

Instead of G-men, we could have T-men. T for Thatcher!

£6m twits

A PACK of civil servants were made redundant and given handsome payoffs.

Then they were immediately **RE-HIRED.**

And the taxpayer kissed goodbye to £6million.

We are not told which twits were responsible.

But they too should be made redundant—without a penny.

The editorial

This is the newspaper editor's view of something. Or it might be the owner of the newspaper's view of something. It is not news: it is opinion on the news. The *Mirror*'s is called 'Mirror Comment'. The *Sun*'s is called the 'The Sun Says'.

▷ On your own, find the editorial in the paper you have and read it. It might be like this:

Britain's litter problem is the worst in Europe – and that's official.
What is the Government going to do about it? It is sickening to walk through all the filth on the way to work in the morning. What must the tourists think as they arrive at our main stations? Why are other European capitals so spotless?
We propose really hefty on-the-spot fines.
We propose children who drop litter should be given extra work – the problem must start in schools.
We propose all unemployed people get to work tomorrow to clean up Britain or not collect their dole.

▷ Write your own editorial on one of the following. Use short paragraphs to make your points.

1 Homework – is there too much or too little for children?
2 Fox-hunting – should it be allowed?
3 Vandalism – how can it be stopped?
4 Playing space – is there enough for the nation's children?

▷ Your editorial in your own paper could use one of the above ideas. It will also reflect any bias you have decided on at your meeting.

Letters to the editor

An interesting part of any paper is the space where the paper's readers give their views. Not all letters to papers are printed so the paper can select the ones it wants to print. Here is a letter:

Dear Sir

I was shocked and horrified to find my three-year-old daughter covered in dog muck after playing in our local park.
I now have the worry of whether she will pick up something or indeed go blind.
I think that all dog owners who let their dogs defecate in parks should be sent to prison.

Yours in shock,

A Worrier

▭▷ Often letters provoke replies. Write a reply to this letter as if you were a dog lover. Write your letter in short paragraphs. Make at least one point in each paragraph.

▭▷ Then write a letter about one of these subjects: Guardian Angels; Hanging for murder; Smoking; Traffic problems; Exams; Fashions you hate; TV. You can use these in your paper. You could also invite members of other groups to submit letters to your paper.

TV, film and theatre criticism

All papers have critics who tell you what they thought about what they have seen (films, shows, videos, etc). In recent years much space has been devoted to TV. Remember when you criticise you can say good things as well as bad. Normally a paper's critic will say:

1 What he or she thought of the story, play, quiz show, documentary and so on.
2 What he or she thought of the actors, presenters, singers etc.
3 What he or she thought of the technical side, such as camera shots.

Here is a criticism of a serial play for children:

● ●

Despite all the money spent on 'Garden Voyage' (BBC1), whispered to be two million pounds, it got off to a poor start yesterday afternoon. The story was too slow-moving and needed cutting drastically. The children seemed too well-behaved for you to believe in them – not a hair out of place or a smudgy face even when chased by a monster. The script did not suit the children and sounded phoney; it suited the adults far better.
I am never very happy when adults dress up as animals and here the make-up of the faces left a lot to be desired.
The best acting came from the wicked queen, although she was inclined to be a bit over the top in the castle scene. Without her performance I would have switched off very quickly despite the superb camera work in the chase by the monster.

● ●

▭ Watch TV or a video at home. Immediately, while it is fresh in your mind, write a criticism of it.

▭ In groups of four or five, find the critics' pages in the papers you have chosen and discuss them, particularly if you have seen the TV show or the film.

▭ You will need to be topical on this so make it one of the last things you do on your own paper.

The magazine part of a newspaper

Much of the modern newspaper is not taken up with serious news at all. It is more like a magazine. Indeed some papers have separate magazines or pull-outs.

▭ Discuss the following in groups of four or five:

1 What would you buy a newspaper for?
2 Are some pieces of news too silly to bother reading?
3 Does the paper you have been looking at cater for your interests?
4 What do you look at first?

In the magazine sections you have things like:

    News of TV soaps
    Cartoons
    Puzzles
    Feature articles about clothes, diet, cooking etc.
    Motoring features
    Horoscopes
    Pop news
    Woman's Page

▭ Search through your paper and cut out for your file the sections that interest you (there are examples below and on pages 123–124).

ANIMAL ANSWERS

by Going Live! vet Nigel Taylor

I seem to have no luck with pets. I've not had a pet longer than a year apart from my tortoise. I had a rabbit but it died of a kidney disease. I have had fish but they died. I had a hamster, a dog, a mouse and a kitten, and now I would really like a dog but I am frightened what might happen. I bought books on all these animals, and my mum and dad have spent a fortune on all these pets.
    Very upset, Birmingham

Oh dear, I'm always very sorry to hear about anyone losing their pets and to lose so many recently must be a real blow. Mind you, I'm sure that if you had a puppy you would be very surprised and pleased to find it's life would hopefully be very uneventful. Make sure that he's vaccinated against the major dog diseases and that he's wormed regularly. Good feeding is important and so is plenty of love. Just in case your dog becomes ill don't forget pet insurance is the best present you can buy your pet.

I have a nine month old border collie. Every time some one goes past our back garden she starts barking. We have had lots of complaints from the neighbours and they are threatening to go to the council. Please could you tell me how to make her stay quiet?
    Chris Pearmond, St Albans.

Border collies are often a bit like this Chris. You see, they're very protective of their territory and don't care much for outsiders at all. You can sometimes overcome it by making a game out of introducing strangers to her on a regular basis and rewarding her with affection when she doesn't bark. All behaviour modification takes time and patience and if you are starting to have neighbour problems have a word with your local vet who can often help.

CARTOONS

Roald Dahl's BFG
BIG FRIENDLY GIANT
Adapted by Brian Lee & Bill Asprey

IT MUST BE A NUISANCE TO BE SO TALL

BONK!

MY BONCE IS GETTING USED TO IT

EXACTLY HOW TALL ARE YOU, BFG?

24 FEET AT THE LAST MEASURING

FEET! NOBODY USES FEET THESE DAYS! YOU MEAN 7.315 METRES!

I STANDS CORRECTED... BUT TELL ME, SOPHIE, WHY IS YOU TWIDDLING YOUR TOOTSIES?

IT'S THESE SHOES - MY FEET ARE KILLING ME!

51/393

FEET? SURELY YOU IS MEANING METRES, MISS CLEVERCLOGS?

AM I RIGHT OR AM I LEFT?

FRED BASSET
by Alex Graham

A ball of wool.

I used to have a lot of fun with a ball of wool when I was a puppy.

I used to toss it in the air...

...chew it...

...kick it...

...shake it..

Yes, I used to have a lot of fun with a ball of wool when I was a puppy.

27/5

123

MIND BENDERS

RIDDLES 'N GIGGLES

WHAT IS THE LONGEST WORD IN THE ENGLISH LANGUAGE ?

SMILES, THERE IS A MILE BETWEEN THE FIRST AND LAST LETTER.

DID YOU BUY THAT DRESS-MAKING BUSINESS ?

YES, I SEWED UP THE DEAL YESTERDAY

WHAT INSECT RUNS AWAY FROM EVERYTHING ?

A FLEA (FLEE).

SPANIEL

WIN THIS WORD GAME BY SPELLING AT LEAST 18 THREE-LETTER WORDS BY USING ONLY THE LETTERS IN THE WORD **SPANIEL**.

AIL, ALE, APE, ASP, ALP, LAP, LIP, LIE, NAP, NIP, PAN, PAL, PEA, PEN, PIE, PIN, SAP, SEA, SIN, SIP AND SPA ARE 21.

MATCH GAME

WHAT MIGHT THEY BECOME ? MATCH THE OBJECTS ON THE LEFT WITH THOSE IN THE RIGHT COLUMN. FOR EXAMPLE: AN EGG MIGHT BECOME A BIRD.

1	SQUAB	A	COW
2	GRAPE	B	FROG
3	MILK	C	PIGEON
4	HEIFER	D	RAISIN
5	TADPOLE	E	CHEESE

SOLUTION: 1-C, 2-D, 3-E, 4-A, 5-B.

4 WAYS TO FLY

PRINT THE PROPER VOWEL LETTERS OVER THE DASHES TO SPELL FOUR WAYS TO FLY.

1	H_L_C_PT_R
2	B_LL__N
3	__RPL_N_
4	SP_C_SH_P

amaze → DRAGON SLAYER

by Dave Phillips

Find the only path that enters the maze, passes through all four swords, and ends in the dragon space, without using any part of a path more than once. You must pass through the sword's hilt first.

124

Reafforestation!

A pegboard and plentiful supply of pegs would be an aid to solving this puzzle. The solution is very satisfying when you find it because of its symmetry.

Answer to Thinks Laterally puzzle: As night-watchman he should not have been asleep to have the dream

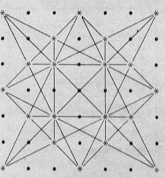

▭ Each member of the group should submit a magazine article for your own paper.

Below and on page 126 there are some examples of work done by people of your own age on their own paper.

SCHOOL DINNERS GOING TO STOP!

You may already be aware that the future of the school catering service is under threat from the Cambridgeshire County Council.

The council wish to operate the school dinner service at minimum levels required by law. This would mean an end to paid meals provided for children and adults by the authority. Instead, packed lunches would be provided for all children who would normally be entitled to free school meals and to teachers carrying out voluntary lunchtime duties.

This proposal is to try and achieve economies in the councils expenditure

This main article was followed by interviews with teachers, dinner-ladies and members of the public.

Outings.

TEN PIN BOWLING IN PETERBOROUGH.

Many people think that because we live in Cambridge the only activities we can do have to be within Cambridge. Young people don't have cars and so can't get to other places easily. People can get into Cambridge by bus, the fares are Appox. ADULT : £1·60 (return)

CHILD (under 14) £0·85p

From Cambridge you can take a train from the Cambridge Station. For a child it cost approx. £1·60 return. (A timetable is enclosed with this).

It is advisable to book a alley before you go. There are 20 alleys at Peterborough bowls. 6 people can go on each alley so it's fun to go with a large group of friend. It cost approx:- ADULT : £1·60 (+ 30p shoe hire)

CHILD : £1·25 (+ 30p shoe hire.)

Going bowling makes a great couple of hours fun.

This illustration is from an article about the coming police checks on bikes.

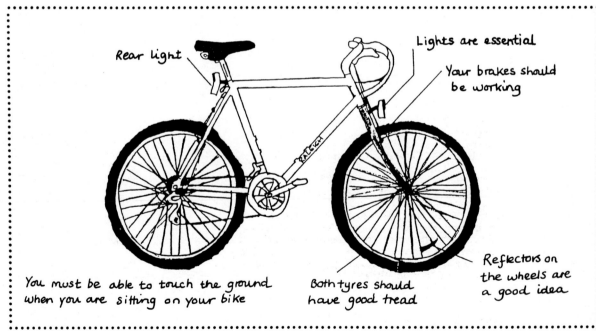

Rear light

Lights are essential

Your brakes should be working

You must be able to touch the ground when you are sitting on your bike

Both tyres should have good tread

Reflectors on the wheels are a good idea

Good luck with your project!
We hope you get some scoops!
We hope your first edition sells out!

Language words

A list of words and terms to do with language follows. Go through them and consult with your teacher about any you are not sure of or have forgotten. The number after the words refers to where they are first mentioned in this book.

Old English (page 10)
Middle English (11)
nouns (11)
capital letters (11)
proper nouns (11)
pronoun (21)
adjective (21)
verb (21)
adverb (21)
conjunction (21)
preposition (21)
parts of speech (21)
onomatopoeia (21)

episode (26)
cliff-hanger (29)
synonyms (33)
subject (53)
plot (62)
simile (67)
rhythm (67)
biography (70)
metaphor (79)
apostrophe (84)
accent (98)
dialect (98)
idiom (104)

LONGMAN GROUP UK LIMITED,
Longman House, Burnt Mill, Harlow,
Essex CM20 2JE, England
and Associated Companies throughout the world.

First published 1991

ISBN 0 582 05517 2

Printed and bound in Great Britain by
BPCC Hazell Books
Aylesbury, Bucks, England
Member of BPCC Ltd.

Acknowledgements

We are grateful to the following for permission to reproduce copyright material: the author, Jon Allen for his poem 'I remember the day'; Edward Arnold for the story 'Bed but no Breakfast' in *13 Ghosts* by Paul Groves; the author, Rachel Brown for her poem 'Friend'; the author, Kerry Carson for her poem 'Mourne'; William Collins Sons & Co Ltd for the story 'Homework' in *Trip Trap* by Farrukh Dhondy; Hodder & Stoughton (Australia) Pty Ltd for the Story 'The Gift of the White Cockatoo' in the collection *The Turtle and the Island* by Donald Stokes and Barbara Ker Wilson (pub 1986); the author, Joanne Holroyd for her poem 'Last Respects'; the author, Elizabeth Macfarlane for her poem 'Brave Soldiers'; Macmillan Ltd, London & Basingstoke, & Michael Gibson for the poem 'Flannon Isle' in *Collected Poems 1905–1925* by Wilfrid W Gibson; the author, Naomi Raven for her poem 'Cherry'; Sole Syndication & Literary Agency Ltd for the article 'The Girl's who can't cope with life after Soap's' in *Daily Mail* 16.11.88; Spike Milligan Productions Ltd for the poems 'Werkling', 'Esquimau' & 'A B' by Spike Milligan.

The authors would like to thank Paul Hindo for his help in preparing Step 3 – 'Our Town'.

We are grateful to the following for permission to reproduce photographs and other copyright material:
BBC, pages 23 and 28; BBC Publications, *Fast Forward*, 122; Beamish Open Air Museum, page 108; J. Allan Cash, pages 25 and 81; Cephas Picture Library, page 116 (Photo P.A. Broadbent); Commercial Union Assurance Company, pages 42–3; Greg Evans Photo Library, pages 44–5 and 60; Mary Evans Picture Library, page 69; Fortean Picture Library, page 57; Sally and Richard Greenhill, page 8; *The Guardian*, page 100; Hodder and Stoughton, *The Turtle and the Island – Folk Tales from Papua New Guinea*, illustration by Tony Oliver, page 88; Hulton Deutsch Collection, page 65; Images Colour Library, page 37 above; *The Independent*, pages 73 and 76–7; Mail Newspapers/Solo Syndication, pages 32 and 123; Mirror Group Newspapers, page 118 left; *The Observer*, pages 75 and 77; PGC Publication Centre, page 9; Tony Stone Worldwide, pages 37 below (photo Zigy Kallizny) and 48 (photo Robert Evans); *The Sun*, page 118 right; Telegraph Colour Library, page 80 (Photosource); Times Newspapers, page 124; *Which Magazine*, page 63.

Illustrated by: Edward Mclachlan, pages 2, 41, 51, 52, 95, 99, 103; Deborah Kindred page 16.

Designed by Jenny Portlock of Pentaprism.